Immigrant Voices
in the Pandemic

Immigrant Voices in the Pandemic

EDITED BY

Roxana Cazan and Domnica Radulescu

 Solis Press

Contents

POETIC REVERIES

DRAMATIC ENCOUNTERS

FICTIONAL JOURNEYS

NONFICTIONAL HYBRIDS

VISUAL EXPRESSIONS

Introduction

THAT THE PANDEMIC AFFECTED the ways in which we live is no longer in need of explanation. From engaging in our daily habits, our social circles, our work environments, to the ways in which we seek a doctor's help, the frequency of our travels, or the way we do business, the Covid-19 pandemic has changed the world from the way we knew it, and a restoration of "old normal" is no longer possible. If explanations of how the new coronavirus pandemic transformed how we live abound, less discussion has been issued around the ways in which the pandemic outbreak influenced how we create art. The present anthology is a testimony to how Covid-19 compelled us to think differently about art's ability to deliver our common humanity, especially in times of global crisis, smuggling stories of immigration, exile, and loneliness into the pandemic frame.

Our first collection, *Voices on the Move: An Anthology by and about Refugees* published by Solis Press in 2020, captured the trials faced by refugees, exilees, and immigrants in an environment rendered precarious by a political ideology of exclusion and demonization of migrants in general. This anthology aims to present the ways in which the Covid-19 pandemic added a layer of peril to the already uncertain existence of migrants. Not only did the pandemic kill over five million people worldwide, but it also brought about a heightened awareness regarding a host of social wounds we must confront and heal for good. From addressing systemic racial inequality or the economic implications of relying on minimum-wage jobs, to the politicization of health care and the escalating mental health crisis, artwork created during this time allows us a more complex view of what it means to be a responsible upstander as opposed to a passive bystander. And this is exactly what we hope this second iteration of this anthology of art and literature by migrants, immigrants, and refugees is able to uncover: that artistic output creates wellness in our lives as it helps us process our lives individually but come together collectively to amplify important messages and deliver hope.

The literature and art included in the current anthology allow their creators and the readers to inhabit a "flow state," that is, to enter a state of focus whose intensity results in ecstasy rather than worry and pain.

First described by positive psychologist Mihaly Csikszentmihalyi, the "flow state" allows our minds' chatter to fade away so that we can reach the limits of imagination and feel fulfilled. Rather than selecting only works of art that directly address the coronavirus or its social distancing antidote, we offer a varied tapestry that weaves in voices on the move, stories of grief and loss on the one hand and recovery and hope on the other hand about topics that the pandemic urges us to consider: home, relationships, culture, identity, language, places, food, memory, and time. We believe that all the pieces included in this collection allow the reader to enter a "flow state," and come out of reading this volume better off.

***

Although unique, our collection is not the only one inspired by the coronavirus pandemic. The anthology *And We Came Outside and Saw the Stars Again*, edited by Ilan Stavans (Restless Books, 2020), depicts life during the pandemic in essays, poems, photographs, and artwork by established artists such as Jhumpa Lahiri, Mario Vargas Llosa, Eavan Boland, Daniel Alarcón, Jon Lee Anderson, Rivka Galchen, Claire Messud, Ariel Dorfman, and others. While most contributions tend to express feelings of hope and connection, some also highlight the despair created by the pandemic and its economic, social, and political consequences. As Lily Meyer writing for *The Atlantic* remarks, the themes of this anthology pendulate between uncertainty and brokenness, despite the brilliant optimism of the line from Dante's *Inferno* which gives the title to the collection. As Dante ascends from his nightmarish visions of the inferno and gazes up to God, he aspires to a cleanliness that would allow him a new beginning. Perhaps Ilan Stavans similarly hopes that the citizens of this earth can also leave behind the tragic hell of the pandemic and begin anew.

The Decameron Project by the *New York Times* and published by Simon & Schuster presents a collection of twenty-nine short stories written by world-renowned authors inspired by the coronavirus pandemic. Like the above-mentioned anthology, it was inspired by a European literary masterpiece written in the fourteenth century in response to the Black Death by Giovanni Boccaccio—*The Decameron*. If this anthology offers compelling and imaginative stories written by established writers such as Margaret Atwood and Edwidge Danticat,

Musings During a Time of Pandemic edited by Christopher Okemwa and published by Kistrech Theatre International in 2020 is an anthology of poems. Another anthology inspired by the pandemic and published by Delacorte Press in 2020 is the YA collection *Together, Apart*, a compilation of original short fiction by nine authors about characters finding love in unexpected ways. Finally the 2022, *COVID Chronicles: A Comics Anthology* by Gene Ambaum, Julio Anta, Ned Barnett, and Ken Best, brings together short comics of diverse narrative styles that highlight the tragicomedy of this global pandemic.

Among these anthologies, *Immigrant Voices in the Pandemic* includes poetry (or the oldest form of storytelling according to Rosemarie Dombrowski), fiction, essay, short drama, and visual art created by immigrant writers as they decipher their lives, their pasts, and their futures, all transformed by the pandemic. As in our previous anthology, the authors gathered in this collection are also diverse: some are well established in their respective fields, others are just beginning their artistic journey; all of their voices come together to compose a choir whose song is audible beyond the pandemic. And, as in our previous collection, all the authors gathered in this anthology are themselves refugees, immigrants, or displaced people and therefore the entire book has emerged from directly lived experiences and personal stories.

The present anthology is equally a feminist work in a wide and layered orchestration, as all authors, who identify differently on the gender spectrum, create intersectional spaces in which the endeavors towards gender equality may intersect with those toward racial, ethnic, sexual, economic justice, and equality. As much authentically feminist art, this collection also opens doors towards social change and equality, or, it is our hope, that in Jill Dolan's words it offers "intimations of a better world." The works gathered here, whether in poetry, prose, drama, or visual arts, innovate at the level of form and aesthetic, create new languages and are often hybrid, thus breaking with traditional forms in all the genres.

"Voices on the move trapped in lockdown" could also be the title of the present anthology. A tragic oxymoron lies at the basis of our book, as it gives voice to stories and experiences lived by refugees and displaced people, normally on the move or in various states of journeying, who were disproportionately affected by the recent pandemic as it has often turned our various nomadic or exilic states into their very opposite: states of entrapment.

***

Our previous volume titled *Voices on the Move. An Anthology by and about Refugees*, traced and explored journeys of displacement, nomadic experiences, traumas of real or metaphoric homelessness and discrimination, survival after loss of home, family, country, wholeness. The book was published in the very summer of the height of the Covid-19 pandemic, at a time when the world was at a standstill, most traveling forbidden, and most humans stuck by various degrees in their various locations and spaces, frozen as if in a sinister game of statues, gasping for air, fighting for life.

The millions of displaced people, migrants, refugees, people on the move fleeing wars, dictatorships, environmental collapse, dire poverty, gang violence, or caught on frontiers, in the limbo of refugee camps, in the act of fleeing, in detention centers, or trapped in small urban habitations with no income and no legal documentation, or with documentation but far from their families and countries of origins, were hardest hit by the pandemic, due to lack of resources, appropriate health care, poor living conditions. The state of roaming, journeying, forced nomadism was turned on its head, into its equally destructive opposite: entrapment.

The present collection has emerged precisely in this passage from dangerous flight to painful stasis of those who carry the burden and sometimes the "bitter freedom of exile" as the Roman poet Ovid coined his state of banishment from his beloved Rome to the "barbaric" realms of Dacia Minor, by the Black Sea, in the first century of our era, in his poignant volume *Tristia*.

While edited collections by new or established writers emerged from the months of lockdown and pandemic agonies, as mentioned earlier in this introduction, some inspired by classical works such as Boccaccio's *Decameron* or Dante's *Inferno*, there are no works that document in artistic forms the challenges and trials of migrants, exiles, refugees during the dystopias of the past few years. This new volume accomplishes precisely this artistic documentation of lives caught in flight, and brought to unwanted stasis or entrapment while equally inventing new strategies of survival, and imagining new possible worlds.

With a heightened level of intensity and tenacity, numerous engaged artists of this and the past centuries have increasingly become like first responders for the violence done to our souls, minds and bodies by patriarchal structures and practices of oppression, thus aiming towards creating through their art processes and strategies of healing. Literature and the arts are not important because they may teach us about history or geography, or politics, which one can learn about by opening the internet or reading a history or political science book, and they are not a self-help or a how-to project, but because they take us on a journey of discovery and self-discovery, because they facilitate understanding about our souls, the world and the human condition and most importantly about those around us. By placing ourselves in other people's shoes, skins, voices, we are capable of living richer, more layered and more compassionate lives.

Poetic Reveries

One thread running through the poems in the collection is a renewed and often fierce clinging to nature, to memories of nature and loved family members, dead and alive, in our countries of birth—attempts to renew our relationship to the larger universe around us and to the intimate universes of our lives, as if restarting the world all over again during the last couple of years. They often focus on women's experiences and the poignancy of motherhood, the difficulties of coping with the realities of entrapment, in pitches that oscillate from dark, to melancholy to bitter self-irony.

Claudia Serea's poems unfold in little agonies of memories of loss and subsequent recoveries, everything sharper and intensified by the doom of lockdowns, the intensity of prime colors framing moments of despair and grief as in the poem "The Year We Stayed Home." The "linden flowers," the "dried mint," "a family of sparrows," are all triggers to the lost native world which seems to exist and pulsate in perfect simultaneity with the moments of existence in the adopted country, and in the silence that has spread over the earth during the pandemic, where the fall of a pear like a "hand grenade" echoes from "5000 miles away."

In **Lucia Cherciu**'s poems the grief over the loss of a dear family member to Covid-19 in her country of birth, or the newly gained habits developed under the lockdown, are delicately processed with memories and gestures of love and kindness, tiny details that acquire momentous significance and are heavily laden with the sense of actual losses, of potential losses, and of the fragility of our existence on earth. The "shiny blue wrapping paper" of the gifts of the deceased uncle, the poet's face in the mirror during a makeshift haircut in the backyard of her house appear frozen in the perpetual present of the pandemic.

Monica Manolachi's poems reveal the agonies and occasional thrills of teenage mothers, "little mermaids," or of refugee women giving birth and mothering alone in the labyrinth of the lockdown. She experiments with form in the superb calligram shaped as a honeycomb, perfectly matching the visual labyrinth with the heart-wrenching realities of stages of motherhood under the pandemic; the entrapment, the desperation, the sinister new ways in which virtual and carnal realities merge and the unhealable loneliness of being a mother trapped in English as a foreign language.

Adela Sinclair's poems continue the unapologetically darker route of nightmarish losses, violence, disappearances of bodies and souls, the agonizing loneliness of "empty streets." Written during the pandemic, they obliquely echo a sense of radical shifts in the relation between the self and the world, a palimpsest of anxieties and visions of the end, and are sprinkled with ironic twists, as in "Nightmares": "Lick your lips, taste the salty crystals,/breathe the apocalypse, as if it smelled of eucalyptus." The present apocalypse sparks triggers to a past in another country, where "brainwashing can last a lifetime," as in "Romanian Poet Watches Unsolved Mysteries Episode 1" and the poet, on her journey in and out of nightmares, wonders "at the end of the tunnel, if there is no light/What then is there?"

Anna Veprinska's excerpt is part of her recently published chapbook from Gap Riot Press. The chapbook offers a rumination on estrangement written from the perspective of a woman struggling with loneliness and with an illness that makes her ever so susceptive to the coronavirus.

With **Julia Kolchinsky Dasbach** and **Luisa Muradyan**'s poems in the series "When the World Stopped Touching," we leap back into the universe of mothers in lockdown, so worn out by relentless childcare all while grading papers or keeping up with virtual work, that parenting inhibitions and rules crumble and wildly self-deprecating humor is the only strategy of survival. Written as epistolary lists and apologies for things done and undone, words said and unsaid during the endless days of childcare while sheltering in place, the poems offer delicious moments of recognition for all mothers who found themselves at home with children and with little help even from benevolent husbands. The humor of the poems is liberating and cathartic through its brutal and necessary honesty as in "Here's a list of things/I'm ashamed of/today alone: 1. Singing fuck/Fuckity fuck fuck/Fuck to all of the dirty dishes/while the baby was strapped to my/back," and is at times coupled with admitting the sadness, the exhaustion, the "bad case of/*the Mommy Blues*, the color of endless water."

With **Annie Lulu**'s poems we move into the dark world of tragic crossings, failed escapes across unfriendly waters, nightmarish flashes of massacred bodies and hostile nature. Amid the darkness and the violence, the ferocious female voice, creativity and will for life trace tunnels of light and hope. Lulu creates striking intersections between female anatomies and natural elements, crosses continents, cultures and languages and invariably chooses "the natural route of what lives, doesn't decay" as in the poem "Kuta (Walls)," all while the poet's body is "stretched by thousands of facets at the eye opening faded by generations" as in "Mambo."

Roxana Cazan's "Ode to a Bellpepper" and "Ode to Hunger," in the tradition of Pablo Neruda's *Odes to Common Things*, remind us with striking intensity of the life of the senses, the carnal realities of foods and tastes that trigger memories of lost native spaces, spices and cuisines, during the cold sterility of lockdowns. The synesthetic imagery of Cazan's Odes, the sensuous gliding in the miraculous world of tastes capture the devouring yearning for visceral realities, "for the round world across the pandemic."

Dramatic Encounters

Ellen Scherer's one-act play "Burning Money," in its beautifully minimalist form unfolds a family drama through the fragments of memory and memory triggers experienced by two Chinese sisters taking refuge in a 1950s' themed diner during the 2021 winter of Covid-19. Through their laconic conversation we find out that both of their parents have died, that their father was a devoted epidemiologist who worked relentlessly during the pandemic while suffering hideous acts of discrimination and harassment due to his racial identity. The sisters' concise dialogue displays a delightfully affective closeness even as they find themselves in what might just be the lowest point of their lives. Traces of childhood blend in with a maturity acquired too fast. The theatricality of this one-act dramatic gem lies in the little gestures that help them pass the time but also contain flashbacks to their family times, such as making pretend money with shredded napkins, and the realist dialogue which oscillates between small talk about popsicles or the weirdness of the diner, to the painful and glaring truth of their private apocalypse: "Come on, Chen. Stop acting like everything's normal! Who gives a shit about tradition when everything we've ever known is just gone?"—a question that probably millions have asked during the agonizing years of the pandemic.

Joan Lipkin's dramatic monologue entitled "Surviving at the A-Ok Convenience Store, Next to the Shell Station off the Highway" offers the reader an intimate understanding of what a recent immigrant to the United States would have felt as they straddled both getting used to being away from everything they knew and the pandemic. Lipkin's character is a Bangladeshi queer woman who must decide how to react to microaggressions perpetrated by individuals about whom she holds her own implicit biases. The monologue invites the reader to reflect on the sources of our stereotypes and the ways in which the pandemic exacerbated some of these stereotypes.

Cătălina Florina Florescu's dramatic piece "Woman, a Choreopoem" takes us inside the lives, psyches, and memories of two women supposedly waiting in an MRI room in a New York City hospital during the pandemic. As the playwright notes: "A choreopoem is a gem, as it is neither poetry, nor drama, but a dramatic expression." Sliding seamlessly between dream, reverie, memory, snippets of reality, and fantasies of a utopian future, the conversations and interactions between the two female protagonists Sun and Renaissance traverse anxieties about their bodies, health, headaches, menopause, sexuality, and are interspersed with humming, singing, and snippets from "episode three of 'What Your Mother Never Told You about Your Health' from The Michelle Obama Podcast." In the last scene, which, according to the author's stage direction, is the only one that happens in real time, as the others happen in "Sun's brain," a complete shift in setting takes us inside a glorious garden in Istanbul where women in colorful robes are drinking the most luxurious tea there is. A photo of Matisse's cut-outs offers a visual cue for the production of the play, which the play-wright comments on at the end of the play, and acts as a meta theatrical commentary on the author's own shapeshifting and collage aesthetic. A fiercely honest and unapologetically female desire for bodily and mental health, happiness and freedom breathes throughout this unique "dramatic expression."

Fictional Journeys

Partly autobiographical, the excerpt written by **Amy Le** is extracted from her novel, *Snow in Vietnam*, which follows the protagonist's extraordinary story of survival as a Vietnamese refugee in an Indonesian refugee camp. Snow, the protagonist, seeks sanctuary in the United States, where she hopes she can find a surgeon to fix her daughter's, Thủy-Tiên's, heart condition. This excerpt offers a glimpse at women's struggles as refugees, where they are tasked with the affective labor of caring for children and the ill, and where they are constantly resisting victimhood as targets of rape, sexual abuse, and discrimination. Although her excerpt does not directly address the coronavirus pandemic, the text situates women as the primary caretakers of the ill and the abused. Snow's precarious position as a woman in a refugee camp is enhanced by the emotional weight of such labor whose only reward is gossip and marginalization. The pandemic offered Le the context to think more intensely about women's position on the front lines, as she developed Snow's fictional journey in the trilogy that followed the publication of this novel in 2020 and 2021.

Neither is **Sandra Soli**'s short story, "Year of the Probable Boom," directly addressing this pandemic, but the pandemic served as background for the writer to consider other worldwide phenomena that threaten humanity with extinction. Hers is a story of an environmental epidemic of sorts, written from the innocent perspective of a child irrecoverably marred by the beginning of the Cold War and the terror it caused. Set in 1953, the story gently nudges the reader to consider the horrific possibility of nuclear war between the United States and the Soviet Union. Soli offers this reminder at a time when Russia's immoral war in Ukraine has created global insecurity. Soli underscores that the pandemic period is extremely complex because it does not solely entail a struggle against a biological virus, but perhaps aided by the insecurities this virus has created, other evils resurface, including the horrendous threat of armed conflict. This story testifies to how the war waged by Russia's megalomaniac leader affects those of us who reside in remote areas outside of Ukraine and Eastern Europe, as Soli's winsome narrator testifies "Images of wet hair, falling out in my hands, converged with pineapples and snow maidens from Paradise in neon dreams that would not wait for sleep, blinking on as I stepped into the shower or began a spelling test." That the threat of war is global remains our take-away from Soli's story.

Alexander Weinstein's short story "Sanctuary" offers a parable, an extended metaphor for how we tend to treat immigrants, especially when pushed to embrace the panic of danger and contamination. The story depicts a highly technological modern world where all activities humans engage in take place through immersive reality. Suddenly, all immersive reality spaces, from game rooms to classrooms or yoga studios, are invaded by extraterrestrials that resemble earthly insects. After a moment of panic where all immersive reality spaces are shut down, humans return to their typical activities. Scientists remark that the extraterrestrial invasion does not represent an attack but a request for sanctuary. Conspiracy theories appear, depicting the creatures as highly dangerous carriers of viruses and contagion. Soon the general population embraces the panic and begins to support movements to exterminate the extraterrestrials, culminating with the president declaring war and inciting all citizens, including the youth, to fight these newly arrived creatures. Some people oppose this abuse and begin sheltering and defending the targets, whose songs "sound like prayer." The story concludes with the realization that "[o]ur visitors didn't need to destroy us—we were doing that ourselves—and the distance they'd traveled was far less than the gulf between us and our neighbors now."

One the one hand, Weinstein's parable "sanitizes" current anti-immigrant attitudes highly sanctioned by the Trump presidency by proposing a science-fiction context where an invasion of extraterrestrials via immersive reality channels seems impossible in real life. On the other hand, however, the story begs us to consider our internal biases towards individuals who look differently from ourselves. The panic rhetoric generated by horrific events such as 9/11 for example, has truly pushed the limits of hatred and xenophobia that we once thought were on the brim of extinction. The pandemic with its manifestations of anti-Asian hatred has revealed once again how eager we are to embrace stories that demonize others and help maintain the us vs. others hierarchy.

Nonfictional Hybrids

"Forbidden" by **Alina Stefanescu** mixes characteristics of lyric essay and reportage. The narrator begins by describing her wanderings in the Alabama outdoors during the period of pandemic lockdown when accompanied by her three children, she happens upon a restricted area that looks heavy with history. At another time, the narrator learns that in this place there used to be a correctional institution for girls deemed untrainable and delinquent. Both the beauty of the physical space completely overtaken by nature and its problematic history constitute occasions for extraordinarily beautiful ruminations on human complexity, gender, survival, and poetry. The narrator concludes with a metatextual analysis that allows readers to consider the capacity of the written word to liberate and to empower: "This essay began with a barrier that felt formal, an inheritance of crossing borders. It progressed through a formal mode, namely wandering, that challenged the essays' linearity by invoking daydreams, unspent similes, strange bells. Now it ends in a space haunted by forbiddenness."

N.S Bala's essay operates on a metaphor of the snake and its hiss to describe the speaker's attitude towards warming up to those around her. Having been mentally affected by the separation from dear ones that the Covid-19 pandemic has imposed, she seeks comfort in adopting an ophidian attitude. What this means, however, is complicated by the writer's cultural background. Bala turns to the Indian classical dance tradition of Bharatanatyam, characteristic of southern India. For the writer, the specific technique and style of this dance resembles the movements and noises a snake makes while expressing intimate and devastating emotions, as the dancer tells a story, usually of separation and seclusion. During the pandemic, the writer returns to thinking about this dance tradition as she struggles with loneliness and longing.

Roxana Cazan's essay addresses the ways in which the pandemic has allowed a different type of conversation on women's rights. Cazan brings together a tapestry of women's voices that tell stories of ostracization, separation, and confinement which stand in contrast with expectations one has of women in the United States in the twenty-first century. Cazan suggests that the pandemic, with its Zoom obsession, has penetrated our intimate spaces to reveal women's position as still secondary to men's.

Written as a generic hybrid congealing nonfiction and dramatic prose, **Domnica Radulescu**'s contribution is titled "Merciless '*Dor*' and My Three Houses of the Apocalypse." As the title suggests, the narrator problematizes the idea of home as an affective space that has the ability to transform. Simultaneously a sacred space, and a space of loss and longing—indeed the Romanian word for longing, *dor*, is used as a lyrical frame for how the writer constructs this space—home embodies a sense of connectedness, of affective agency that the world struggled to understand over the years of this pandemic. While Radulescu ties the idea of home to the physical space of a house, the narrator's three houses are not physical structures. Although they are composed of physical elements, they sketch an affective landscape of belonging that is as much made as it is given by one's mere accident of birth. In fact, Radulescu's piece suggests that despite the pandemic, one—even a perpetual migrant—can still find a sense of safety, of courage, and of resilience in their own affective conception of home, one's surroundings, and one's memories. By defining the "social" and the "historical" as always affective, Radulescu's contribution aims to "redistribute the sensible" as Jacques Rancière suggested, in that she demonstrates that art, particularly writing, can offer new possibilities for perceiving the real world through aesthetic experiences of memory, landscape, and text. These aesthetic experiences have a political impact, crucial at a time so alienating as this pandemic has been. They produce a multiplicity of connections that allow one to reframe one's relationship between one's body and the space it occupies and the possibilities of a literary text to embody.

Rajiv Mohabir's essay is a version of a keynote talk he delivered at the "Live Pridefully: Love and Resilience Within Pandemics" organized by the Caribbean Equality Project on June 24, 2021. Mohabir wants the audience to understand that survival for the queer community of color, particularly in the context of the pandemic, is a complexly layered gesture that requires the privilege of "moments of respite and community." In fact, Mohabir argues, survival rests at the very root of queer Caribbean identities. Like N.S. Bala, Mohabir also draws on Indian mythology by referring to metaphors of resilience in the face of homophobia, transphobia, or general hatred and violence. His message centers family and community survival within the context of the physical and social devastation during the pandemic.

Visual Expressions

Octavio Quintanilla's visual poetry combines media to produce a unique message. A watercolor collage, his poetry sends a clear message: a call for help issued by a voice that represents a multitude and who implores an unresponsive interlocutor to allow the speaker to see. The metaphor of lack of sight may be Quintanilla's approach to dissecting the consequences of the pandemic, this virus robbing humanity of one of its primary senses and leaving it without a trajectory for adjustment. His poetry however also utilizes Spanish, his mother tongue, which invites the reader to expand their world view to include those whom the pandemic excluded from public narratives in the United States: migrants, immigrants, indigenous, and Latinx communities whose access to a quality life has not only been curtailed by the pandemic itself but also by centuries of white power and privilege.

Likewise, **Najmeh Hoseini**'s oil paintings center the issue of race and ethnicity by alluding to real events. These events not only have taken place during the period of pandemic lockdowns and restrictions, when social frustration and anxiety reached a zenith, but also underscore the need for social justice through restoration, restitution, empowerment, and antiracism.

Finally, ΔURΔ etc echoes back to Quintanilla's work, referencing the fragility and ephemerality of life during the pandemic and in general. By focusing on the body, the artist illustrates the need to understand all bodies as equally precarious in the face of the pandemic and other devastating evils, such as war, authoritarianism, fundamentalism, or neocapitalism. Notwithstanding the artist's location in proximity to Ukraine today, a space devastated by a cruel war waged by a megalomaniac leader resembling Romania's own communist dictator—the artist's home and location are in Romania—ΔURΔ etc's artwork invites us to reflect on our shared humanity and on our capacity to survive and learn.

Poetic Reveries

Claudia Serea

The Year We Stayed Home

It was the year when I built you a house of clouds
and filled it with thunderclaps and summer rain,
so you could sleep well at night.

It was the year when I raised a house of dough,
kneading love that sticks to fingers
and swells in the oven,

a home of cake scent and crunchy walnuts
that reminded me of my mother's,
assembled from *fursecuri* and croissants.

We lived in a grandfather clock
where the seconds and days ticked away
like ants across the floor,
carrying the crumbs of our lives
into the charred forest.

It was the year when I almost lost you,
even though you were right here,
in the nest of my placenta
and its amniotic liquid
where we both floated,
unseparated at birth.

It was the year when you wrecked your body,
and I built a house of screams
in which you wailed and hated me,

the year we cried
on both sides of the bathroom door,

when I cut open my ventricles
and made a quivering step ladder
so you could climb back from the ledge.

It was the year when I grew a garden
of red tulips in a blue vase
on a black table
against a yellow wall.

See, we can make anything with love,
I said. And you believed me,
and took my hand.

Sunflower Season on Instagram

I hold the yellow light by its stem
and take photos.

Around us, the whole world
strikes a pose and clicks away.

You bring your face close to the open corolla,
touching its golden lips.

Thinner than a sunflower stalk,
emaciated, you keep smiling.

One more photo,
one more.

At home, I hide my worries,
undress the disk from its spent florets,

uncovering the toothy seeds.
I roast them

and sprinkle them with sea salt,
food for girls and birds.

We split them in our teeth
and spit out the empty shells.

The Hand Grenade

When I set the teapot on the stove
and prepare the linden flowers,
or the dry mint leaves you gave me from your garden,
I think of you.

I think of you when I go for a walk
and look at the cloud hanging over the Passaic River,
its belly full of cold rain,

and when I watch the family of sparrows
on the telephone wire.

My hand holds the phone
and I think of you
when I hang up without calling.

At night, my thoughts move inside the dreams
like chicks rustling in the eggs
set in the incubator in your kitchen.

Their wings feel for flights that aren't there yet,
not this year.

This year is grounded.

In August, slowly,
slowly,
slowly,

in your orchard 5,000 miles away,
a pear separates
from its branch

and falls through the air,
heavy,

before smashing on the ground
like a hand grenade.

And my heart,
in this cursed year,
does the same.

Lucia Cherciu

Blue Wrapping Paper

For Vasile Diaconu (1954–2021)

Sometimes I wrap an empty box in shiny blue paper. I remember
the surprise. When I had nothing, I knew how to appreciate everything.

Somebody had cut a branch off the fir-tree and brought it inside.
That Christmas my uncle brought me candy and chocolate

wrapped in royal blue paper. I try to remember
what kind of chocolate it was. The gifts over the years.

This March, he returned to his house late, too sick to make a fire.
The ambulance came, carried him to three different hospitals

that couldn't take him. Then the tests confirmed he had Covid.
Finally, one hospital kept him. The family was not allowed to visit.

His discharged phone. We stayed up late praying, tethered to hope.
My mother kept the lights on all night, called us and cried.

On the wall, the picture he gave me some twenty years ago.
The photographs he took bring back places forsaken, dreams renounced.

I wrap an empty box in shiny blue paper, fold the edges back,
smooth them out, try to remember what kind of chocolate it was,

what kind of candy. I try to remember the last day I saw him,
almost three years ago. Have I praised him enough? Have I told him

how his gifts brightened our childhood? His countless forms
of generosity. In order to remember hope, I look at the picture

of wild hawthorns that he gave me. Sometimes
I make a list of all the gifts he brought over the years. Sometimes

in a store, some shiny blue wrapping paper arrests me
and I remember the child's anticipation of joy.

Prayer for an Apricot Tree

The apricot tree deliberates whether to come back to life
or not. A dormant tree shipped across the country in June.

In Romanian, apricots are feminine, grapes masculine,
and apples neuter. Gender is a matter of language.

Every morning when I water the apricot tree, I check to see
if a green leaf has broken. Abiding respect for trees that return.

Even the roots were trimmed down, bare. The chance journey
of trees that travel from a nursery across the country.

Does the tree learn the name of the person who planted it?
Recognize my voice? The warning of things that burn.

The floorboards in the living room. My chair, the windowsill.
Are they still alive? Do they still remember?

The triumph of an apricot tree that takes. I ordered it online,
and it has a one-year warranty, but I would have to ship it back

if it dies and I don't see myself going to the post office
with a pack of dead sticks.

He's not dead, and I'm not sending him back. I remember
all the trees my father planted. He picked apricots,

laid them out on the table in the good room and saved them for us
when we went home. The longest it's been since I didn't go home

is three years. Last year my daughter didn't want to go to Romania.
This year is Covid and the whole world is learning how to pray.

In two months, since we moved to this new house,
we have planted eleven fruit trees, including two figs.

Slowly, our garden is coming alive. Slowly, I learn to open
the gifts passed down to me. Slowly, I learn to share the fruit.

Haircuts in the Backyard

My husband combs our daughter's hair in our garden,
then trims it. He is precise and gentle.

When my turn comes, he measures to check if even.
Though fading off, the red dye still strong. The gray

comes through. I color it myself, refuse to pay
the thousand dollars it would cost a year

to get it done at the salon. Coloring it at home
makes the house stink with toxic chemicals,

makes me nauseated. I've frittered away my youth.
How much time did I spend fiddling with my hair?

When I catch a glimpse of myself in the mirror
I see my mother. I worry she will say I look old.

My husband combs my hair in our garden.
Besides our daughter, in Adirondack chairs,

my grandmothers and great-grandmothers have joined us,
their long, gray hair shining, rinsed with walnut leaves.

Monica Manolachi

Little Mermaids

Fancy living in a city inhabited just by teenage mothers,
each on her own, without any of their family support.
Imagine living there for a year and during that time seeing all
of the mothers and their babies cry for milk, tremble with cold,
some of them starve to death. And not so much school time.
You do have enough food, clothes and toys for everyone.
And there is only one of you. You are the architect, the builder,
the doctor, the fireworker, the judge, the mayor, the police officer,
the priest, the singer, the teacher, all of them at once.
But they are helpless teenage mothers with one or more babies,
thousands of teenage mothers, cradling their newborns.
You race frantically from young madonna to young madonna
and never sleep, never stop to eat and drink, never go to the toilet.
I am one of these mothers. Did I want to become one?
In my grandparents' yard, the first apple to ripe was mine.
When I was small, my parents brought me a red toy TV,
a musical automaton with three dancing ballerinas inside,
in blue tutus, with delicate overhead *port de bras*.
Then they departed, taking planes to different destinations.
I was counting the streets and the cars, the trees and the doves,
hoping they might return, hoping to show them my homework.
One summer holiday, I met a duende, half boy, half goat,
his voice was changing and I found it so hilarious!
He brought me rivers and hills, the moon and the stars—
I lost control, lost sight of myself, lost punctuation.
To be a woman is freedom without choice, the nanny goat
warned me, to be a woman is language without voice.
While flocks of starlings were crossing my mind,
I wished I could turn back time but I never could.
Birch trees grew inside me and I was alone in the forest,
nowhere to go, knowing nothing, with no one to help me.
I am sitting here, in this fictitious city, trying to answer
why we all started so early, but I can hardly figure it out.
Those newspaper pictures and those extensive reports
rarely seem to capture the smiles of our babies.
I may be that number in the government statistics,
but I am also a brave girl, life-loving and reliable.
You'd better do something for your little mermaids!

Blue Honeycomb

Childbirth cannot
be put on pause, so she
is picturing the little face
in the dark, skin to skin, the
faint heartbeats. She wishes she
had a doula to keep her cool,
but some hospitals force
women to labor alone.

She has been on a
furlough for some time
now. Her boss is paying her
wages, but her lover is paying
too much attention. Insecurity,
boredom, hits and bad jokes
and the urgent desire to
lock the door and
swallow the key.

He sends
message after message
and calls her wife over
and over. The front desk is
busy all the time. So he bakes a
tray of oat flapjacks as if the
dead could ever return from
the woods of medical
vocab.

Those grooming
remarks. Those gory
images. That guitar sound.
Trying to escape online harm
when there is no escape: bully or
be bullied. Gone without
eating, gone without sleep.
Tied hand and foot with
social ropes.

On Blursday night,
the film falls silent as
the virus infects her laptop,
blending actors' dialogues and
pupils' voices in her mind. Next
morning, when spreading
cheese for the kids, the
teacher hallucinates
zoombombers.

His mother has
been waiting between
the fine lines of borders,
brushing the wavy hair of
memory, without complaint.
She taught him how to speak
with foreign winters. When
he comes back home,
she heals him without
request.

She has collected
words, long and short,
like swords in a panoply.
Looking beyond the borders
of the photographs, she can now
show the difference between
immigrant and refugee,
crisis and tragedy.

She was the age
of today's youngest
mothers. Her first poem
was about a rainbow, each
color having something to say,
in rhyming couplets. That arc
is now bridging dark totali-
tarianism and a puzzling
democratic regime.

I am a bee in this
huge labyrinth, a bee
in the shape of a woman,
trying to compare and contrast
patterns of loss and gain, wondering
about being or not being a
bee, in a language that is
not my mother's.

Adela Sinclair

Romanian Poet Watches Unsolved Mysteries Episode 1

All it takes is an empty street.
This is what I fear most.
Not the ghosts, demons, nor angels
I saw at the age of twenty-three.
    They taught us in school: everyone
    must do their jobs.
    The way entities overtook me.
    After all, even our teachers.
    Brainwashing can last a lifetime.
    Before the garbage cleaners
    will dispose of the trash.
All it takes is an empty street.
Were there any witnesses
at the Belvedere Hotel
in the middle of that night?
His body dropped
through the ceiling
into the conference room.
An accident? How was it
geographically possible?
His bones shattered.
The courtyard was empty.

I am afraid of what they will find.
Everyone who saw it shuts their mouths.
I am afraid stamina means
staying where you are not wanted.
The ones who are vindictive
do it in ways you cannot imagine.
    All it takes is an empty street.
    I am at the window looking out.
    Mother, you've told me one too many
    secrets.
    Your words are the window.
    You are the window.
    I shatter with understanding.

    So what if I smelled the blood first?
    We are all born bloodied.
    Isn't there enough liquid
    for the world to get wet?
    What wants out must be birthed.
    Sometimes bridled.

    Holding the sparrow in my hands
    the words flush out.
    A mural of headlines, confessions and verdicts.
    You've told me one too many secrets.

The witnesses at the Belvedere
all followed the same script.
They lied with authority and conviction.
Nobody saw his body fall
nor be pushed
off the roof of the hotel.
The hole in the ceiling
his body fell through
still there.
Gravity was faster than him
he could have changed his mind
on the way down
falling,
falling deep under.

Nightmares

The commonality of nightmares chills our blood.
The common denominator is the body,
the messages within our flesh, our organs,
throats letting out yells of terror then constricting.
Say we did away with nightmares.
You and I would kill.
Say all life became unworthy of our interiors.
Not worth analyzing, nor reflecting upon.
Repression happens.
Even to the most ardent truth teller, suppression.
We do not need to be in touch with our shadow selves.
We must just allow our shadow selves to be in touch with us.
Fabricating conclusions is not your place as the poet.
Opening doors for all of us doormen becomes our civic duty.
Nightmares suffice.
Potency to release our darkest fears from our paths, the living.
We mustn't be afraid of such things.
Remember for us, you matter as much as what you release.
Let us have a bonfire to burn all that is stuck,
bottled up, untimed, latent, unblossomed yet.

We're forced to be whatever we resemble
Vivre et laisser mourir,
move away from fear,
end the lies.
A windy day and the bridge swings under your feet
and the kayakers pursue their dreams, sliding among
frozen spots on the river.
At the end of the tunnel, if there is no light,
what then is there? You leave your box, crawl out of it,
and journey into finding out. Defying a tragic ending,
à la Marcel Duchamp, you don't take the stairs while
being followed by intruders. It happens. When
you've been saved once or twice, you start to owe back.
You cannot become blood kin,
for your blood's no good. Genetically speaking, you'd die
before the fall. The stairs are covered in a *bleumarin* rug,
Marcel Duchamp's head dangles off the bottom step,
his body, a sketch stretched out, a figment of a life.
Let them laugh, their time will come!
Flesh out your steps.

You are the devil she proclaimed you to be!
They will laugh at your horns made of branches,
and the red lights caressing your face. Take out the menu,
and the red lights caressing your face. Take out the menu,
order from the profundity of your being. Lavish
your body, the expert of letting go.
Proust's madeleines are stale by your bedside.
Lick your lips, taste the salty crystals,
breathe the apocalypse, as if it smelled of eucalyptus.
Tragique they say, of your death.
Confront the light, no more song and dance.
De sang froid, they say, of your murderer.
We're all forced to be whatever we resemble.

Anna Veprinska

Spirit-clenched[1]

[Walls]

Walls so thin
we disease

the neighbours. Illness
sieves
as water

through tea leaves. We
bequeath fever
and the fleshy

longing
of prayer.

[Land]

Land
perforated with

theft, as fleshy
at wounding—

this cleaved
terrain, this tender

edge
of not yours.

---

1 Both excerpts are from *Spirit-clenched*, Gap Riot Press, 2021.

Julia Kolchinsky Dasbach
and Luisa Muradyan

From "When the World Stopped Touching"

April 29, 2020

Dear L,

Here's a list of things
I'm ashamed of
today alone: 1. Not holding back
my hand from my son's
lips the third time
he spit on me. 2. Throwing
one toy away and lying
about the other. 3. Drinking
a spiked seltzer, while playing
mama and papa
cars on the floor, filling
the toy dump truck
with goldfish and letting
the baby shove them,
fists full, into her mouth
covered in cat and dog
and human hair 4. Taking
another, long sip. 5. The second
I considered what would happen if,
while washing the dishes,
I just stuck my hand
inside the running disposal.
How much damage
would it really do? Enough
for a few hours in the ER
or longer? Enough to keep me
from ever playing the guitar or holding
a pen, my children or just enough
for a break 6. Remembering
today's my grandparent's
fifty-eighth anniversary, but not

believing my Babushka
has ever been in love.
Loving my children
is enough, she says.
7. For me, it isn't.
8. Saying, *Do whatever you want,*
but I'm not talking to you, my mouth
full of my mother. And yes,
my son cried and yelled, *But I want*
hug and kiss! in broken Russian.
I know you hear me! He strapped
his arms around my waist,
hung me with all fifty pounds of him.
It only took minutes, L,
for him to be breathless
with tears. I hate myself.
9. For the minutes
I didn't hug him back.
I swore, I'd never do it.
The stone on my chest.
My mother's lessons.
This was her preferred way
of getting me to listen.
10. If he becomes a father,
I'm afraid this is what
he'll pass on, not my hands
or words, but their absence.

April 29, 2020

Dear J,

Here's a list of things
I'm ashamed of
today alone:
1. Singing fuck
Fuckity fuck fuck
Fuck to all of the dirty dishes
while the baby was strapped to my
back. 2. Telling my toddler
that the world will be healed
soon even though I don't

know if I'll ever see his hair
bounce through every aisle
of the grocery store ever again.
3. Grabbing my husband's
butt when I thought the children weren't
watching *they were*.
4. Letting my son watch *Frozen* for the nine thousandth
time and then letting him watch *Frozen 2*
for the eight thousandth time.
5. Crying in the middle of dinner, to which
my son replied, *mommy is a little bit sad*
today. 6. Being a little bit sad today
7. Getting baby poop on my pants in the morning
8. Not changing the same pants until the afternoon
9. Letting the baby cry longer than I should have because
I had to finish grading a paper.
10. Grading papers too slowly when I should have
finished them weeks ago.
11. Ignoring my toddler until he threw his plate
against the wall for attention 12. Putting my screaming
toddler in time out even though he just wanted my attention
13. Giving my toddler attention

May 7, 2020

Dear L,

My husband wants me to stop
asking how he's feeling, startled
by his every groan or crack
or heavy sigh, *Stop asking*
what's wrong, he says. *you know*
what's wrong. And I do L, to list
the ailments would take
too many lines and far
too much worry I promised him
I'd try to quell. But aren't we
made of it, L? Worry
passed down from my mother
who I call more times a day
than I have children, every
morning and every night, no matter

the hour or else she assumes
something terrible has happened.
In her mind, it's always terrible
until my voice reassures her
I'm still here. Worry, burned,
inherited in flesh: my lips
and wrists, my collarbone, the backs
of my knees, under my breasts,
volcano, he calls my body,
loving and fearing it
at once, worries I will burn
him too. He was coughing
the way a fire starts, smoke
rising from the basement,
the sound of his chest, his throat
tearing open like the gut of fish
or the belly of a hunted doe.
I crept downstairs, silent, until
the coughing stopped and I
snuck back up to bed, not asking
a single question, but wondering if,
after ten years of marriage, a lifetime of unspoken worry
is something we can bear.

May 9, 2020

Dear J,

I'm worried that I worry too much
worry that son A isn't kind to son B
and that son B will internalize all of the
stolen toys and shoves and seek his
vengeance on son A and really
I've barely spoken to my brother in years
so what do I know about forgiveness?
I am desperately trying to learn
from the women in my family
who will forgive you before you've
done anything wrong. And J
this is beautiful and terrible
and dangerous and what I am saying
is I'm worried about the murder hornets.

May 9, 2020

Dear L,

Happy Mother's Day! I simply
had to write you that today
I wanted nothing more than to be
away from my children, from myself
as their mother, from everyone celebrating
us as though we are doing anything
more than what we have to. I love
my children the way I hunger.
But no one has ever celebrated
you for not starving, for being full.
We are mothers to desire first,
but after, it's mostly momentum.
So when my son yelled, "Happy
Movie Day" instead and daughter
bit down on my nipple, laughing
at my tears, I kept going, L,
mother, just another name
for constant motion.

May 11, 2020

Dear J,

My favorite genre
of Mother's Day gifts
is the clever coffee mug:
Tired as a Mother, M(aster) O(f) M(ultitasking),
Volleyball Mom, Soccer Mom, Hockey Mom,
Dance Mom, Dang You're Always Right Mom,
World's Best Mom, Best Mom Ever, Best Coffee Drinker
Mom, I went to Florida and All I Got Was this
Coffee Cup Mom, Boy Mom, Girl Mom, Llamma Mamma,
Little Mom of the Prairie, Mother of Dragons, Mommy Dearest,
And my personal favorite, *Home is Where the Mom Is.*
And J, this year's mug was wrapped in a grocery bag
light pink with red letters
Mom, est. 2017 written across the handle.
It was the year I cried so much I could
have flooded each cup in the cupboard.
A therapist told me that it was just a bad case of
the Mommy Blues, the color of endless water.

Annie Lulu

Kuta (Walls)

Kwa[1] Aminata Dramane Traoré
À propos des corps morts en mer Méditerranée

I believe my cousin's brother swallowed a mouthful of water in a blue sea
one could say he's my brother's brother
one could say he's my brother
home, everybody has some brother's brother
dead trying to join the world's death side
while it's the place you'd rather be fleeing
the tiny typhoon sucking up all the dead corpses of the world's life
it's the place you'd rather be fleeing
My cousin's brother, his brother, I mean my brother
even though I am his brother's cousin, that is to say his cousin,
never told him that one dies a lot amongst the living dead
that one must be of a species of men damnedly altered to eat death,
where he wanted to go,
that living with those men is like killing oneself,
you can become like them
destroy murder smear like you breathe
just by doing your shopping cooking watching a movie
I don't understand
why want to die in death when you can do it much later and in life?
I think my cousin's brother, my brother's brother, my brother
he didn't have a compass
I mean a reliable compass
of those that won't push you towards:
other people's life
other people's money
other people's sea
other people's god
all their endless shit
and an organ traffic farm on the way
That is why I was lucky, I took the opposite route

---

1 The author draws on her Congolese–Roma–Romanian and French identity. *Kwa* is a
  reference to a group of languages spoken in Congo. *Kwa* can also be read as *qua* on
  one hand but also as a reference to the Francophone world—*editor*.

the natural route of what lives, doesn't decay,
since my compass is a normal compass
it points South.

✳✳✳

je crois que le frère de mon cousin a bu la tasse dans une mer bleue
on pourrait dire que c'est le frère de mon frère
on pourrait dire que c'est mon frère
chez moi tout le monde a un frère de frère
mort en voulant rejoindre le côté de la mort du monde
tandis que c'est ce lieu qu'il faut fuir
le typhon minuscule aspirant tous les cadavres morts de la vie du monde
c'est ce lieu qu'il faut fuir
le frère de mon cousin, son frère, je veux dire mon frère
même si je suis la cousine de son frère, c'est-à-dire sa cousine,
ne lui a jamais dit qu'on crève beaucoup chez les morts-vivants
qu'il faut être d'une espèce d'hommes sacrément altérés pour manger de
    la mort
là où il voulait aller
que vivre avec ces hommes-là c'est se tuer,
tu peux devenir comme eux
détruire assassiner salir comme tu respires
rien qu'en faisant tes courses en faisant à bouffer en regardant un film
je ne comprends pas
pourquoi vouloir aller mourir dans la mort quand on peut le faire bien plus
    tard et dans la vie?
je pense que le frère de mon cousin, le frère de mon frère, mon frère
il n'avait pas de boussole
je veux dire une boussole fiable
de celles qui ne vous poussent pas vers:
la vie des autres
l'argent des autres
la mer des autres
le dieu des autres
toute leur merde infinie
et une ferme d'organes en chemin
c'est pourquoi moi, j'ai eu de la chance, j'ai fait la route inverse
la route naturelle de ce qui vit, ne moisit pas,
puisque ma boussole est une boussole normale
elle indique le Sud

Mambo

Kwa Margaret Walker Rituel

with the *ngenguba* picked today
I bead a seed necklace
bourbon stones instilled with the heavy sugar of a bloody mint julep
the jewels that I craft are old rums
smelling around the camshaft that has become my fable
beading, memory of the mints
tying, rolling up to the central alveolus
hexagram navel
my body stretched by thousands of facets at the eye opening faded by
generations
my sporulated pearls at the ankles of the trees
ah, that I am the woman!
larynx of my land splendor of the seedlings' justice
mother
aunt
artisan mambo with equator sparkles
saluting with my fingers the Stars of the Hip
song of songs nested in a shell
of closed branches
tight
each time we found the agrobate
digging into the deposits of my throat's delta
each time a trampling coucal crossed out my stride
ah, that I am the woman
the perimeter of the *sorgues*
the belt of one more night
because tomorrow will be early
and the sky hasn't yet conquered the farandole of constellations
which serve me as a yawn
my people's pillow oozes full flames
—*okei wapi, moto?*
—*likambo na yo te*
the stars *na yo te*
the moon *na yo te*
nothing *na yo te*
bandeke, where will you be burning then?

✳✳✳

avec le ngenguba cueilli jourd'hui
je perle un collier de graines
rouges et noires comme le lait des mères
pierres de bourbon instillées au sucre lourd d'un *mint julep* ensanglanté
les bijoux que je fabrique sont des rhums vieux
odorant le pourtour d'arbre à cames devenu ma fable
perler, souvenir des menthes
nouer, rouler jusqu'à l'alvéole central,
nombril d'hexagramme
mon corps tendu par milliers de facettes à *l'ouverture des yeux*
évasé par les générations
mes perles sporulées aux chevilles des arbres
ah que je sois la femme
larynx de ma terre splendeur de la justice des semis
mère
tante
mambo artisane aux scintillances d'équateur
saluant de mes doigts les Étoiles de la Hanche
chant des chants nidifié dans un coquillage
de branches closes
serrées
chaque fois que l'on a trouvé l'agrobate
creuser les dépôts du delta de ma gorge
chaque fois qu'un coucal piétineur a biffé mes foulées
que je sois la femme
du périmètre des sorgues
de la ceinture d'une nuit encore
car demain sera tôt
et le ciel n'a pas encore vaincu la farandole de constellations
qui me servent de bâillement
l'oreiller de mes peuples suinte des flammes pleines
—okei wapi, moto ?
—likambo na yo te
les étoiles na yo te
la lune na yo te
rien na yo te
bandeke, où brûlez-vous alors?

Taa (Light)

Kwa Euphrase Kezilahabi
en regardant par la fenêtre

work,
barely dressed in pads of sad paws
of the frozen birds on the opposite roof
my work belongs to the impossible flight
related to what belongs to something
I toiled, I threw my fruits at the near thaw,
stunned bitter gourds, acrid, cooked and pearled like my period
in solar spikes in upturned lips
irradiated by the acescent love, kneaded in the urine of the days,
caustic *girembelles* stuck in my diseased kidneys
with their clots starred by a thousand promises of men,
and my only monkey bread
and for nothing
all my labor now transient
my fruits frozen by the waiting
the dead birds' bodies stranded in the yard
in a thousand pieces of stemmed glasses

✳✳✳

besogne à peine vêtue des tampons de pattes tristes
d'oiseaux gelés sur le toit d'en face
mon travail appartient à l'envol impossible
au lien de ce qui est à quelque chose
j'ai peiné, j'ai jeté mes fruits au dégel proche,
margoses assommées âcres cuites et perlées comme mes règles
en pointes solaires en lèvres retroussées
irradiées par l'amour acescent pétries à l'urine des jours,
girembelles caustiques coincées dans mes reins malades
aux caillots étoilés par la dispersion de mille promesses d'hommes,
et mon unique pain de singe
et pour rien
tout mon labeur est transi
mes fruits glacés par l'attente
les corps des oiseaux morts échoués dans la cour
en mille morceaux de verres à pied

Roxana Cazan

ode to a bell pepper

it's amazing how there's a stream of color
es asombroso cómo hay una corriente de color
running through you, warped like time
in this pandemic, around the beveled bell,
deformado como el tiempo en esta pandemia
and hollow like a refugee's pockets
hueco como los bolsillos de un refugiado
the world around you and your brother
handselled with *algunos momentos de toque íntimo.*
hemos olvidado como morder la carne,
we have forgotten how to season and spice,
hemos olvidado como condimentar,
once upon a time, in a village,
with cinnamon and jicama,
con canela y jicama,
how you, the sweetest most bitter
sun casting your rays of unpolished copper,
how you can bring me to tears
when I taste my mother's gentle touch
pruebo el toque suave de mi madre,
lighting up my torn world,
iluminando mi mundo desgarrado.

ode to hunger

this poem is an appetizer
as savory on the tongue as *zacuscă*
everything I can swallow:
this poem is like watermelon & feta
brightened by a single sprig of mint
from a garden in my other country
where everything kept growing
despite the personal distance
like in a bed where sleep is sweating miracles
I want to taste that which fits on my plate
what is sweet   what is risen
my baby's milk-sour breath
what my body has enough of   but not everyone
is made of the same hunger
here in Oklahoma my kitchen bulbs blister
with light despite the ice storm
I stay put   I hunger
for the round world across the pandemic

Dramatic Encounters

Ellen Scherer

Burning Money: A Play in One Act

Characters

BAO: seventeen, very bright and strong willed. A true gem.
CHEN: fourteen, very superstitious. Can be timid but for good reason.
These characters are second- or third-generation Chinese Americans.
They should not have a Chinese accent for the hell of it; only if the
actors genuinely have an accent.

Setting

1950s themed diner; February 12, 2021.

At Rise

BAO and CHEN are sitting on the floor next to an old space heater. It's
freezing. They're stretching their winter coats and scarves between the
two of them, creating one makeshift blanket to sit on and another to
wrap around themselves. BAO is reading the graphic novel, *Fun Home.*
CHEN is sucking on a lollipop while reading over BAO's shoulder.

BAO: Could you not do that?
CHEN: What?
BAO: Read over my shoulder. You always do that.
CHEN: No, I don't.
BAO: You do, but whatever.
CHEN: Sorry.
BAO: Where did you get that?
CHEN: Found it in one of the pockets.
BAO: Which one?
CHEN: I think it was the right one?
BAO: No, I mean … Which jacket?
CHEN: Mine. I think.
BAO: Hmmm

CHEN: It's good. Want some?

BAO: Ew. No.

CHEN: Alright, fine. More for me.

[*Beat.*]

Hey, B? How long do we have to stay here?

BAO: Ugh. I don't know. But complaining about it isn't gonna make time go any faster.

CHEN: I'm not. I'm just wondering when—

BAO: I don't know, okay? If we're lucky, we'll get out of here in the morning.

CHEN: Okay.

BAO: I think there's a YWCA in the next town over. This place creeps me out.

CHEN: Same. There's this weird energy. Can't put my finger on it.

BAO: It's probably the whole 1950s toxic nostalgia vibe.

CHEN: Do you think it's bad luck?

BAO: No, it just sucks.

CHEN: The decor *is* a bit much … Wow, check out this mural over here. What would you even call this?

BAO: A Hopeless Devotion to Poodle Skirts

CHEN: Hahahaha …

BAO: Literally the only good thing about the 50s was the obsession with milkshakes.

CHEN: What about the drive-ins?

BAO: Okay I'll give you that. But this place? We wouldn't even be allowed to sit down let alone order a milkshake.

CHEN: Probably not.

BAO: Look who's laughing now…

[BAO *goes back to reading,* CHEN *looks around, trying to figure out what to do next.*]

CHEN: I'm gonna go check the register.

BAO: cái yuán gǔn gǔn[1]

CHEN: Thank you!

[*Beat.*]

Wait. You're being sarcastic, aren't you?

---

1   "May a river of gold flow into your pockets."

BAO: Yes. I'm being sarcastic.

CHEN: Why are you so grumpy?

BAO: We're hiding out in an abandoned diner during the fifth apocalypse of the year and you're looking for cash to burn?

CHEN: It's tradition!

BAO: Like that matters.

CHEN: It does.

BAO: No it doesn't. Nothing does. It's all bullshit. All of it.

CHEN: What?

BAO: You heard me. Come on, Chen. Stop acting like everything's normal! Who gives a shit about tradition when everything we've ever known is just gone? Dad's gone. He's gone and … burning old paper bills isn't going to bring him back.

[*Beat. BAO has been holding this in for some time and maybe starts crying.*]

CHEN: No. It's not. But that's not the point.

BAO: I know. It's just … This isn't fair. We got so much shit over the past year. We lost mom, we lost the apartment and Dad put up with so much fucking shit before he——

CHEN: ——I know——

BAO: ——Was it not enough that every day on his way to work as an EPIDEMIOLOGIST he had people yelling hateful racist shit at him through their car windows? Was it not enough that when his car was in the shop and he had to take the subway, people would run away from him or throw their hot coffee in his face because they were scared the color of his skin would give them the virus?

[*Wipes away her tears.*]

Was it not enough that he put his entire heart into studying this pandemic? He had to let it take his life too?

CHEN: Bao, you don't mean that. You know he did everything he could to hang on.

BAO: I know. I know he did.

[CHEN *doesn't want to push it., but she also doesn't want to give up.*]

CHEN: You're right, B. It's not fair. But something tells me we're gonna make it through this.

BAO: What if it never gets any better out there?

CHEN: It will. It will.

[CHEN *gives BAO a hug. The girls just sit together for a moment.*]

I'll be right back.

[CHEN *disappears into the back of the restaurant.*]

BAO: [*to herself, wiping her tears away*] So much for "stability" and "calmness." Stupid ox. [*To* CHEN] Hey, let me know if you find any pink ladies back there!

[CHEN *comes back. She has a big stack of paper napkins stuffed in a coffee can.*]

CHEN: Very funny.

[CHEN *sits back down next to* BAO. *She dumps the napkins on the floor.*]

Look what I found!

BAO: Paper napkins?

CHEN: To the untrained eye, yes. These are paper napkins. But to an artiste like myself …

[CHEN *tears the napkins into strips and blots them with her lollipop to give them some character*]

Dollar bills!

BAO: [*laughs*] Amazing! I can't believe you found all that cash just laying around back there.

CHEN: I'm choosing to think it's good luck.

BAO: Here, give me some.

[CHEN *hands* BAO *some napkins and* BAO *proceeds to tear them up vigorously.*]

Wow, this is actually pretty therapeutic. Got another lollipop?

CHEN: No, [*digs through her jacket*] but I do have a pen!

BAO: Hello $1,000 bills! How many should I make?

CHEN: As many as you want.

BAO: I'm thinking the higher the bills the higher the honor.

CHEN: I don't think Dad's gonna care.

BAO: You know it was never real bills, right?

CHEN: Yes, B. I'm a big girl now.

BAO: [*laughs*] I'll never forget the look on your face—

CHEN: You said you were gonna burn my allowance! And dad got so mad … he stormed in all—

BAO: "Stop running around like a lunatic!"

CHEN: "It's joss paper. It's fake! For burning, not buying." And then I locked myself in my bedroom for two hours to find a new place for my piggy bank.

BAO: You didn't trust me.

CHEN: You're damn right.

[CHEN *starts digging through her jacket pocket for a lighter.*]

BAO: What about now? Got your piggy bank secure in there?

CHEN: [*smiles*] Shut up.

[BAO *looks around the abandoned restaurant.*]

BAO: Jeez. This place really is an eyesore …

CHEN: At least it's covered in red.

BAO: Hmmm. Yeah. Maybe it's good luck, after all.

CHEN: Our unexpected protection.

BAO: Our temporary stability.

CHEN: Hear that? Take a hike, nián shòu[2]!

[CHEN *hands* BAO *her lighter.*]

Care to do the honors?

BAO: I'm … I'm not really sure what to say.

CHEN: How about … Xièxiè[3]?

BAO: Xièxiè, dad. Don't worry 'bout me.

[BAO *kisses the bill before lighting it on fire and dropping it in the coffee
    can.*]

Wǒ xiǎngniàn nǒ[4]

CHEN: We both do.

[*Fade to black as the girls continue to light their makeshift joss paper.*]

THE END

---

2   A beast in Chinese mythology that lives under the sea or in the mountains.
    According to legend, Nián Shòu attacks Chinese villagers around the Lunar New
    Year. The "Year Beast" is afraid of the color red, so people decorate their homes
    with red lanterns and scrolls for protection.

3   "Thank you."

4   "I miss you."

Joan Lipkin

Surviving at the A-Ok Convenience Store, Next to the Shell Station off the Highway

I thought I was afraid in the old country. To be a girl that looks like a boy and afraid to be found out. Then along comes the virus. But this virus for a queer Desi Muslim is a different thing, here where I am living now.

I thought when I came here, I had landed in heaven. Women driving. Grocery stores with much food. Blue jeans and tee shirts. Blue jeans!

Oh, and Rap music.

And anyone can go to school. Did you know that? To the community college.

Well, it costs money but anyone can go. Not just rich people and men.

I thought, this is the chance for a better life. Not just the one I was born to or the one that was chosen for me. No, maybe I can study. Maybe I won't get married off and have babies and work in a stall like so many women in my village.

All things are possible through Allah. Even this.

I can't believe my parents let me go but they knew I was different. I sometimes heard them talking about me late at night. They were afraid for me. They thought I might be safer someplace else. And I used to beg and beg to go to school. It was my favorite thing.

I was never interested in girl-things or girl-clothes. In girls, yes. But that came later. And that was not safe, either. So, I know they worried.

We didn't talk about it. We don't talk about such things where I am from. But they could see.

So, what a thing to come to America, after many, many months and conversations and documents. You have to have those documents.

I came here because I got sponsored by my uncle and his church. They have this special program: Resettle the Immigrant.

I had to write an essay and they chose me! Can you believe it? And because my uncle is here, and could keep an eye on me, my parents said yes.

I said I wanted to study and know more. How things work and how to help people. I want to learn and make a contribution.

I got sponsored through my uncle and his church and enrolled in the community college. They helped me find a little apartment and buy me a bed. There are cracks in the walls and bugs crawling around so I mostly sleep in all my clothes.

At night, I sometimes hear gunshots but it is the first time I have my own room and a lock on the door. I am grateful to these church people. One of them helped me get a job at a store not far from where I stay. A-Ok Convenience. Do you know it? Next to the Shell Station off the highway.

I am hearing about this virus like everyone else. People say, stay home. Stay inside. But I have no choice. I have to go to work.

Just like the bus drivers and the nurses and the janitors. We are the people who keep things going.

I ask my boss, "Can I work the third shift, stocking, so I will not be around so many people?"

Because people are coming all day.

Chips. Tobacco. Coca-Cola. Oh, and lottery tickets. Lots and lots of lottery tickets.

Usually, I like to work the first shift because I can practice my English more but now I want to be safer and around not so many people.

He says no, my boss. He says so few people are coming to work, he has to move me around wherever he needs. First shift, third. Stocking, cashier.

I say, OK, even though I will miss the classes I am taking on my tablet, the one the church gave me. First, I got to go to class. I was a real college student. My uncle even got me the tee-shirt. But then, with the virus, it was all about the tablet.

I mean, the church helped. But I still have to work. And to be an immigrant, is to have things changing under your feet all the time.

I work with Mohammed. So that is nice. He doesn't say much but still, it is nice to be with another immigrant and a Muslim. Sometimes I see him looking at me, and I know he is wondering things, but he does not say.

People think you are stupid when you don't speak English well. But you know, it is like a secret weapon. Me not speaking English so well, that is. Because I am listening all the time and I am understanding in different ways.

I understand about vaccines. In Bangladesh, my country, they are giving vaccines to children so they won't get polio. Even in the small villages like the one I am from, mothers are proud to take their babies to the clinics to protect them. They tell everyone and celebrate. We have stopped polio because we are doing the right thing.

So, I don't understand here. Why so many people hate the vaccine. Why they won't get it.

I want so much to get this vaccine. I can't wait for it to be here, for people like me, working at the A-Ok.

And this guy, this Dr. Fauci, is my hero. I can see kindness in his eyes and how determined he is to keep going. His voice is hoarse from talking so much. He is older than my grandfather and yet he keeps going. What a man.

I cut a picture of him out of the newspaper and taped it on my wall to cover the big crack. I look at it every day, next to the pictures of my uncle and my mother and father and brothers and sisters and cousins.

"Wear the mask," he says. "Wear the mask, wear the mask. It is one way we can stop the sickness."

Oh, and this thing they call social distance.

I hear him and I am ready to do my part.

But people come into the store, and they are not wearing the mask. They are not keeping the social distance.

I ask my boss. He shrugs. I want to ask what he thinks about this, but he is so tired. Half the time, we are out of things or people don't show up to work.

I ask where Mohammed is. He says, "He is sick."

He was my friend, Mohammed. My only friend at work and a Muslim like me. My boss wears a small cross on a necklace and likes cheeseburgers that he heats in the microwave.

In my country, we eat rice and drink tea, especially seven-color tea.

So many things I miss about my country. My mother and father and my sisters and brothers and cousins, yes. But we talk on the phone when we can, and they are happy for me.

They are so funny. They ask if I have met any movie stars yet. They don't understand that this is not the land of movie stars, here, where I am at the A-Ok.

Sometimes, I think the hardest thing is the language. I miss speaking Bangla. I listen to music from home and read poetry in Bangla, but I get so tired, and not just from just working at the A-Ok. It is speaking and listening in English all day, trying to think in English. My brain gets tired, trying to get it right.

When I sleep, I dream in Bangla. I try to hold onto my dreams where I am in a green, green field and I hear the sounds of my people all around me like music. But I often wake up when someone is yelling or I hear the gunshots. I don't know who they are coming for or why they are so mad.

It is a very scary time. I go to work and then back to my apartment. I leave my apartment and go back to work, no stops. Well, maybe the grocery to get rice and vegetables once a week or to the church where they are giving out food.

I am so grateful for that church. They hand out things I never had before. Things like Cheerios and this thing in a can called Chef Boyardee. My uncle really likes those, the cheese ones.

I wear a mask I bought at the Walgreens and I wash it in the sink every night.

Last week, I got some extra to bring to my uncle and his family but I couldn't go because he has Covid. So, we Facetime.

He says, "You didn't come all this way to get sick. You have to be strong. Wear your mask. I want you to do good for the family. You are the smart one, you are special."

We don't talk about how I am, that I am a girl that looks like a boy. We don't talk about such things. It is not our way. But he knows. He has seen photos of me when I was little.

Once, he said to my mother, "She looks like a boy. Like she could be your son."

My mother got mad. She said to him, "But she is not a boy." And he said, "Well, she's different. And she is smart. Allah does not make mistakes."

I love my uncle. He is always there for me, and I can depend on him being in my corner.

But it's hard. I don't feel so smart. No, no, not so smart. And I am lonely here without my family. I miss my mother's cooking, especially her *bhuna khichuri* with *dim bhaji*. The fruit trees full of mangoes and jackfruit, and waking up to the sounds and smells of our village. Even the chattering of the magpies.

I don't tell her. I don't want her to worry. About how alone I feel, about the gunshots and about the bad people who are here.

Like one day at the store, several guys came in, drunk. They were wearing red hats that say MAGA on them. I backed away because they were not wearing masks.

The tall one got mad. Maybe he was mad because we were out of toilet paper. I don't know.

Then he put a six-pack of beer on the counter and said to me, "What are you looking at, boy? You know you Chinese are the ones that brought this damn virus here and now you're trying to take away our rights."

I told him, I am from Bangladesh, in southern Asia. It is not China.

I didn't say the Chinese didn't bring this here like Dr. Fauci explains because he was standing very close and his face was red. His eyes were red. Everything was red.

He said very loud, "Are you talking back to me, boy?" and shook his finger at me.

I said, "No, no. I am sorry."

I wondered where my boss was with so much shouting going on, but he was in the back with the TV on, doing inventory. He likes this show I think is called *The Price is Right*. He wears his mask but it is usually under his nose. I don't correct him, either.

It is a strange thing. I am supposed to be working on my English but also not say things. Not ask questions or tell someone they are wrong.

My heart was beating so fast. There were four of these guys in these hats. If they don't pay, it will come out of my paycheck?

I asked if they needed anything else? Cigarettes? Lottery tickets? Candy? "You want a Snickers bar? We got Snickers."

He smiled, and slapped a ten-dollar bill on the counter. "Keep the change, little buddy," he said. "Since you are not from China. But lose that pussy mask."

They left, and I felt like crying. But I didn't. I have to stay strong. For my uncle and my family. I had to finish my shift.

And OK, I am angry, too. Why do I have to always be nice? I think they are paying me to be nice. It is part of my job. But I think they also expect me to be nice because I am from somewhere else. An immigrant. Like I should be grateful to have them yell at me because I get to be here.

No, no.

Sometimes, I wonder, what was I thinking to come here? When do I get to study like we planned? When can I make friends or meet people like me?

There are so many people drinking and being mean. There are people living on the street here, too. And begging. Like at home.

But here, here, there are also gunshots at night.

I am scared a lot of the time. But I don't tell anyone. Especially my uncle. I don't want him to worry.

And I know there are doctors and nurses and teachers and scientists here, too. And nice houses with yards and flowers. I have seen them on the bus and at school when I first got to go.

I want those things. No, what I really want is to be those things.

When I got home, I Facetimed my uncle and told him only good things. That someone gave me a tip for good service today.

He said, *"Alhamdullilah*—thank God," and that he needed to go back to sleep. I tried to do some of my homework online but I was so tired, I fell asleep, too.

As I was falling asleep, I thought, if we ever get out of this, this pandemic with the Covid, I am going to become a famous scientist like Dr. Fauci, who everybody knows. I am. I will have a girlfriend and speak English so well, everyone will want to hear me. I will not be afraid. And when someone is wrong, I will say what is on my mind. I will tell them many things about this time.

Or maybe I won't say anything.

Cătălina Florina Florescu

Woman, a Choreopoem
(or, That Time when Michelle
Obama & I Had Da Hong Pao Tea)

Dedicated to all the men in my life.

Statement: This is a choreopoem dedicated to its originator, Ntozake Shange. In 1975, she coined the term while she was working on her brilliant piece, *For Colored Girls Who Have Considered Suicide/When the Rainbow Is Enuf.* One of the reasons why I teach this play is because the author did not compose it exclusively in the rigid, white, restrictive King's English. The play has far more merits than this, but for a woman who takes a lot of pride in her Balkan English added to the still not fully accepted, nor even promoted in the academia Englishes, I humbly thank authors like Shange who, indirectly, give me visibility, too.

A choreopoem is a gem, as it is neither poetry, nor drama, but a dramatic expression. During the tragic year of the pandemic, I realized that I had to start anew and refuse to return to old habits. Thus, I have been experimenting a lot with my own dramatic expressions. As Shange envisioned, a choreopoem has poetry, dance, music, and song. Personally, I treat definitions as invitations that may be explored. Admittedly, some are fixed and smelly, and can't embrace change (like misogyny, or capitalism). Others are playful (like woman, or choreopoem). As such, my choreopoem will expand its original usage by introducing one photo in which I play with a pair of scissors. I am definitely ready to cut and release myself. I am tired of my old bruises.

If woman is a fugitive that's bc, like language, she's never fully done—*necoaptă.*[1]

---

1   From my own poem, "Portrait in Syllables & Mixed Languages," dedicated to Ntozake Shange and published here: www.linkedin.com/pulse/portrait-syllables-mixed-languages-ntozake-shange-florescu-phd/. *No* edits shall be made to this motto.

Characters

SUN: mid-forties, womanist.
RENAISSANCE: late fifties, icon.
Several projections of female-identified humans.

Setting

The longest year of our lives/the pandemic year. An MRI room in a New York City hospital/A tea garden in Istanbul.

Note on Characters

SUN is a tribute to all the glorious female identified humans in my life. Once in a blue moon, I feel that some words could have been said by me in *real* life. Maybe I even said them. It's still too blurry.
RENAISSANCE is actually the Secret Service nickname for Michelle Obama, the former First Lady of the U.S. of America. She is a fantastic woman.

Note on Structure

This choreopeom is made out of scenes. Therefore, there are no acts. There is no intermission. Everything happens seamlessly. When the two characters want a break, they close their eyes and breathe.

Note on Setting

Except for the last scene, everything happens inside SUN's brain. The room has the stillness of a hospital. But SUN and RENAISSANCE will make it come back to life. On other occasions, it should be still. Women like silence if and only if *they* decide it's time to rest.

Note on Quotes

When RENAISSANCE's lines are typed in bold and with quotation marks, those are taken from episode 3, "What Your Mother Never Told You about Your Health" from The Michelle Obama Podcast. If such indications do not exist, then it is an imaginary/imagined First Lady.[2]

---

2   https://storage.googleapis.com/pr-newsroom-wp/1/2020/08/WOMENS-HEALTH_RENAISSANCE_TRANSCRIPTadbreaks.pdf

Ideally, the voice of Michelle Obama is highly recommended, since that will enhance the choreopoem's impact significantly.

The second poem incorporated in this choreopoem was originally published in *The Blue Nib Magazine*.

Let us take the shoes off, quiet our minds, and enter.

Scene One

[SUN *is seated to be wheeled inside an MRI machine. She assesses the room playfully. She hums. She closes her eyes. Darkness. We feel that darkness as it has multiple layers. Darkness, as in its literal meaning. Darkness, as in inside a woman's body, especially her intimate parts. Darkness, as in a consequence of outdated words and attitudes that plague a society. Darkness, as in a starless night. All of a sudden, we hear a sound, the light appears, and* SUN *is wheeled back from the MRI machine. She sighs, relieved.*]

SUN: [*Seated, clearing her voice*] A … LONG … DAY.

[*One more time.*]

A LONG DAY.

I went for a long walk

and reached the end

of the Earth. It was

full with

rinds

and I wanted

to bite into one

you know

just for fun

or thirst

or maybe to pass

the time

because it was getting close to bedtime:

I needed to feel

Something

on my tongue.

[SUN *reaches for a glass of water. She drinks quietly. One may not have access to such an item in that particular space, but we are in an imagined hospital, and that glass is an ordinary prop. How clever, right?*

Hence, she will not be seated the whole time. But she will be inside that room almost until the end.]

SUN: I came here reluctantly. What can this MRI really observe? All these machines that measure our bodies translating it into numbers, symptomatology, charts … [*Shivers*] rigid. I even made a bet with someone I love. I told him, "Fine, fine, you drove me nuts." [*Stops, laughs. Looking very directly to the audience*] What?! How do *you* love? Love is crazy. Love is fulfilling. Love is … indefinable. "Fine, fine, you drove me nuts," I said, "If you insist with this nonsense, I will go. I will go and have that goddamn MRI." "Your headaches have worsened." "I am *exhausted*. That's all." "Please go," he said. Now, you don't know him … he is very kind. And I have no idea why I did that.

…

[*The scene ends abruptly. Her space is closed by a hospital curtain.*]

Scene Two

[SUN *is not seated. She holds that glass of water and then tries the water playfully (e.g., with the tip of her tongue; with a finger submerged in the glass and then brought back on the tongue; she gets closer to smell the water, even if it is odorless). Then, she pours water through her fingers and let her paper gown get wet. She sighs, somewhat satisfied. Suddenly:*]

RENAISSANCE: Are you OK?

SUN: Who said that?

RENAISSANCE: Turn around, so you can see me.

SUN: No! What? *No*!! Is that really you?

RENAISSANCE: I'm next.

SUN: Where?

RENAISSANCE: Inside that [*points to the MRI*].

SUN: Unbelievable. Can I …?

RENAISSANCE: What?

SUN: Can I hug you?

RENAISSANCE: Only from a distance. You know, C-19.

SUN: Yeah, I forgot.

RENAISSANCE: Of course. I *forget* that, too.

SUN: Another time.

RENAISSANCE: Excuse me?

SUN: That hug.

RENAISSANCE [*Determined*]: No way! Make the most out of every single second! So, let's hug. [RENAISSANCE *stretches her arms and tells* SUN *to do the same.*]

SUN: That was fun … To hug from a distance.

RENAISSANCE: Live and learn. Live and enjoy. [*A beat*] Was that painful?

SUN: What?

RENAISSANCE: That [*points again to the MRI machine*].

SUN: Piece of cake.

RENAISSANCE: What kind?

SUN: Chocolate.

RENAISSANCE: Yummy.

SUN: But European style.

RENAISSANCE: What do you mean?

SUN: Syrupy.

RENAISSANCE: Duh! I was the first Lady… I should have remembered that. Although… those years … I had to be perfect. To be liked. To pose.

SUN: And now?

RENAISSANCE: Now I'd like that syrupy chocolate cake so I can finally enjoy it. You know: **"I have changed, and tried to adapt, and I've been accommodating, I've accommodated my husband, I've accommodated society, I've accommodated my children, now I'm done. Whew."**

SUN: This is why I love you. [*Embarrassed*] I mean … Oops.

RENAISSANCE: Don't oops me! Don't write off your feelings!

SUN: Fine, I love you. I thought it was too soon.

RENAISSANCE: Too soon for … ?

SUN: That statement.

RENAISSANCE: Women waste precious time trying to find the [*makes air quotes*] perfect moment.

SUN: I have a sister.

RENAISSANCE: How nice!

SUN: She is not here.

RENAISSANCE [*Matter-of-factly, but kind*]: I can see that.

SUN: She is back home.

RENAISSANCE: Home?

SUN: Romania.

RENAISSANCE: I have never been there. That syrupy chocolate cake must be from that place.

SUN: Or Europe. Europeans know how to cook. [*Sighs*] Why are you here?

RENAISSANCE: I can't sleep. And I don't want pills. Or apps. But my girls insisted. "Mom, is that time …" "That time for what?" "That time to take better care of you … your body …" I was waiting, you know, to see, will they be saying, "aging," the forbidden word for women? They were smiling knowingly. "Look at you, smarty pants, all grown up … Fine, fine, I will go … since it's *that* time … you know … when your mother faces the beginning of her end …" That silenced them! [*A beat*] Why are you here?

SUN: He said, "You should have an MRI." My headaches started to become a nightmare. I have no idea why I did that.

RENAISSANCE: Come here?

SUN: No. …

[*The scene ends abruptly.*]

Scene Three

[*SUN sings and dances. The music stops and SUN is frustrated.*]

SUN: Play that song again. I loved it. [*A beat*] Hello? Fine, I can make my own music!

[*SUN starts to make noises by clapping. She uses her hands against various parts of her body to produce more sounds. She adds other sounds with her voice. Some kind of jam session rhythm is created. She is happy and starts to spin. RENAISSANCE enters and joins SUN in her spinning. They hum together. They stop. They giggle.*]

RENAISSANCE: You know … I think I can't sleep because I'm aging. I asked my mother about menopause. She was like, "What???" and I was like, but really only to myself, "Oh, my God, she must be losing it." I mean … you know … it's hard … to see your parents aging … drifting away … sleeping more … melting in front of your eyes. I remember: **"My conversation with my mother, you know, good ol' Marian, I love that, I love that woman, 'cause she talks about a lot of stuff, but then, there's just some stuff she's like I don't know, I don't, I don't remember menopause. I was like you don't rem– Ma, you don't remember it at all? Can you give me some hints,**

did you have hot flashes? Ahh! Which, you know, and she's eighty something, so, you know, look, I barely remember what I did last week, so, I mean maybe by the time I'm eighty I won't remember menopause either, but that is, another reason why we need to talk about it, while we're remembering it. Our friend group, we've had many, many conversations over the last ten years or so, about menopause."

SUN: How lucky!

RENAISSANCE: Perhaps. Not remembering, you know … some parts of life …

SUN: How lucky to still have a mother.

RENAISSANCE: Oh, no! I am terribly sorry. If I knew …

SUN: Same outcome. [*A beat*] I think your mother is right.

RENAISSANCE: Is she?

SUN: We need to devise a system and forget the non-essential.

RENAISSANCE: Like … maybe half of it?

SUN: At least. What's your favorite song?

RENAISSANCE: I have too many, based on moods.

SUN: Where are you right now?

RENAISSANCE: In a hospital.

SUN: Duh!

RENAISSANCE: Exactly, duh!

[*They giggle.*]

SUN: I meant emotionally.

RENAISSANCE: I knew that. I was just giving you a hard time.

[*We listen to Snoh Aalegra, "I Want You Around."*]

SUN: Do you think they will wait for us, outside of this room, take this paper gown off of us, touch us gently, dress us up? Do you think they will do that?

RENAISSANCE: Who?

SUN: Our men.

RENAISSANCE: I came here alone.

SUN: Me, too.

RENAISSANCE: I'd rather not.

SUN: No?

RENAISSANCE: I mean … there is a time for sex and there is a time for *our* intimacy. And now, since I've reached *that* time, remember my girls? I think I am in the mood for me.

SUN: Self-discovery.

RENAISSANCE: Exactly.

SUN: I know what you mean. I did not want to come to have this MRI.

RENAISSANCE: Sometimes is good to be scared. I mean to face what scares us.

SUN: It is not that.

RENAISSANCE: OK.

SUN: I knew if I came they could not find why I have these terrible headaches. These machines would not pick on my real longing …

RENAISSANCE: Do you need some water?

SUN: I'm fine.

RENAISSANCE: We need to be alone sometimes. Do you want me to leave?

SUN: No.

RENAISSANCE: Great, because I would not have left you. Listen, woman to woman … all real. When I was in the public eye, I could not say everything that was on my mind. One time: **"I experienced the night sweats, even in my thirties, and, when you think of the other symptoms that come along, just hot flashes, I mean, I had a few before I started taking hormones, I remember having one on *Marine One*. I'm dressed, I need to get out, walk into an event, and, literally, it was like somebody put a furnace in my core, and turned it on high, and then everything started melting. And I thought, well this is crazy, I can't, I can't, I can't do this. Any person who's going through menopause who's going to work every day in a suit, you can be drenched in sweat, down to your core, in the middle of a freezing cold office, and have to shower, and change clothes, and fix your hair all over again."** It *really* helps to know when to hide our secrets and when to be as clear as day.

SUN: I did not want to come here because … No, I can't.

RENAISSANCE: Make time for *you*. If you want to say what's on your mind, you *will* say it. Trust me.

[*The women resume humming. They stand up and mirror each other's moves.*]

Scene Four

[*SUN and RENAISSANCE are seated on their backs. In V.O. we hear SUN at first. Then, when the poem is over, they look at each other. We lis-*

ten to the poem one more time, but this time both women recite it by mirroring each other. There is an ad hoc *choreography. As they move, the lights change to pastel colors.*]

SUN [*Voice-over*]: RAW, IN REVERSE

Playing with a fork on a barely touched meal he sighed.

She didn't say a word—Took a sip of water.

He tried again

to eat.

"This tastes like shrapnel."

A war lasts longer after it's declared over. She looked for something underneath the table. "I need air."

She put on a diver's mask.

By the time she was at the door

the whole place disintegrated under water. On second thought, A post-card from a distant galaxy.

[SUN *and* RENAISSANCE *say it again. Recited together, the poem is actually transformed. As they do that, we see projected the photo mentioned in the playwright's statement.*[3] *There are no directorial indications here.*]

RENAISSANCE: What was your mother's favorite song?

SUN: Johann Strauss's *Radetzky March.*

RENAISSANCE: Awesome! I should add it to my workout list. [*Smiles*]

[*We listen to that piece and both women clap, feel the rhythm in their undulating bodies, and are ecstatic. We can sense their energy and will reciprocate.*]

RENAISSANCE: I just realized … I mean I have a healthy baseline, but I see, I feel, I can't ignore that I'm aging. [*Annoyed*] Those super-heroine myths!

SUN: I thought this was part of the American psyche!

RENAISSANCE: That gotta change! We should have never fallen for that childish, male perspective. [*Shakes her head*] Women … women do the hard work: homework with their kids, barely sleep, cook, clean, go to work, go through bodily changes … I mean … even if some are not mothers. Women … some of us *bleed.*

---

3   Please refer to the photo at the end of the script.

Scene Five

[*Reprise from Scene 3. We hear in V.O.:*]

SUN: *Do you think they will wait for us, outside of this room, take this paper gown off of us, touch us gently, dress us up? Do you think they will do that?*

RENAISSANCE: *Who?*

SUN: *Our men.*

[*A moment.*]

SUN: For the longest time I have struggled to be *fericită*. Not for a second, not for someone else, but for me. I don't care anymore if, when I open the door, he is there or not. I told him … *I-am spus* … I will take a vow of silence. The ball is entirely in your hands. To let go is the hardest thing for me. To let others plan for me is probably a first. Maybe I do want to be on the Moon, feel imponderable, and all that. If we happen, we happen. *Să fim fericiți.* [*A beat*] During the longest year of my life, I have had my own revelations. All I need is: a change of clothes for each season, my sneakers, a bed, a stovetop, a fridge, my books, a bathroom, a table, a chair, reusable cutlery, and … [*taps her forehead*] and … my *passport*! Everything else is … [*realizing it is irrelevant, she stops*] I have tried for the longest, and you know what? [*Looking at* RENAISSANCE] Do you like tea?

RENAISSANCE: Yes.

SUN: Let's have Da Hong Pao.

RENAISSANCE: Isn't that …?

SUN: The most expensive? It's not even half of what we deserve.

RENAISSANCE: Shouldn't we wait for our results?

SUN: Nah, we are fine.

RENAISSANCE: Let me make a phone call.

SUN: Let him wait.

RENAISSANCE: It's date night.

SUN: What does that even mean?

RENAISSANCE: You reconnect.

SUN: Aha … In Romania, date night means one thing.

RENAISSANCE: Let me guess … to be in her pants?

SUN: Yep.

RENAISSANCE: And she?

SUN: …

RENAISSANCE: What does *she* want?

SUN: She has no idea.

[*SUN tears apart her paper medical gown. RENAISSANCE does the same. They wear vibrant, beautiful robes. We transition inside a tea garden full with women all dressed up in silky, pastel robes. We hear a rustle. They drink the most expensive tea in the world and are fully relaxed and happy. They are in Istanbul, one of the few cities that spreads its "legs" on two continents.*]

Scene Six

[*All the women from the previous scene surround SUN.*]

SUN: I was inside that hospital room, letting an MRI machine look inside my brain. *I knew why I hurt so much.* [*Puts her hands in front of her face because even retrieving screams from a woman's body and mind is reliving them. This is a flashback*] "I'm not going! And that's final!" "You are impossible!" "And you are so last minute … When I need you, you are silent." "You knew …." "What, that you were silent?! It was too late. I had already fallen in love with you. Do you even know that I had to supplement your lines in my head, so I do not feel so lonely, so that you, you, you, still have a meaning for me? GET OUT OF ME! OUT! NOW! [*Opens her eyes. Does not want to be in pain anymore. Different tone*] Have you ever heard of *precision* medicine? Fucking hilarious! As if humans have anything precise and … permanent [*A moment*] I knew that if they dared to cut me open instead of examining my brain, I would be only water. I would reincarnate as a tiny fish swimming towards finding *me*. Inside that machine, I kept hearing my entire life's screams and cries, now exiting my being.

[*A moment.*]

So many women started to bake sourdough bread when the pandemic hit. I don't enjoy being in the kitchen, so I didn't try that. But my grandma … she loved tea and bread. She wouldn't discard the bread, not even when it was stale. She would make croutons or French toast.

[*Breathes in. Breathes out.*]

When this whole nightmare started, I had no idea why it hit me so hard. It took me an entire year to figure it out. It was the smell of the sanitizers everywhere: on surfaces, on our bodies, in the air, in discourses. Our intimate spaces resembled hospitals. That was it!

[*Breathes in. Breathes out.*]

Mid-pandemic, I have started to have more and more dreams. They were full of people. They were vivid dreams. They had so many details, long dialogues. Sometimes, if I am being frank, I'd wake up exhausted. Yet, I did not feel alone anymore. Like this one time, I was with *Michelle Obama*. Un-freakin'-believable! We were talking about our bodies. We were talking about transitions. During the pandemic, I realized that I had to face the deadly virus and my peri-menopause. *Everything* was shutting down! I could not ask my own mother and trace our intimate map together. She died young. I did not want to upset my older sister because she wanted to have a second child when early menopause hit her in her thirties. So, Michelle and I laughed and we cried and we danced and we decided that our top priority is our bodies and syrupy chocolate cake. One time, she said, "[s]exuality ties …"

[*RENAISSANCE enters.*]

SUN: No way! Was this real? [*She is deeply moved; possibly cries*]

[*RENAISSANCE nods and mouths "Is real."*]

RENAISSANCE: **"[s]exuality ties to other things around health. Mammograms, pap smears, all of that, is like, if you're, if you can't touch your breast, because you feel like you can't, you'll never discover a lump earlier, if you're not getting regular Pap smears, you're probably not going to the doctor, at all, right, so, our comfort level with our sexual health is directly tied to our, in my view, our physical, overall well-being. And I don't want my daughters, to think that they can't ask questions when something is wrong, when there's a bump, or a lump, or a, you know, something out of sorts, if we've shut them down sexually, when they're young, it's their first interaction, as adolescents, with health. And, if we shut that down, what does that do to them later on in life, when they really need to be questioning when things feel different, when things are wrong, when there's a discharge, when there's an itch, when there's a, all of these are signs of bigger things that have to be dealt with, but if you've shushed that, that conversation, in your household, for girls and probably for boys as well, you're shushing down the power that they'll have, in the years to come, to have control over their health, to take control over their healthcare broadly."**

[*RENAISSANCE takes a seat.*]

SUN: Everything came back *to be ended*. There I was: in another cold room, clothes off, *measuring* my health, reminiscing on all my mammograms, pap smears, blood pressure and blood tests, when I started to laugh. I laughed so hard, I must have peed my underpants. After my mother died, one day, I was on the floor, bottle of liquor in one hand, lit cigarette dangling from the corner of my mouth, listening to some sad songs, when I started to laugh hysterically. My dad came to check on me. "Are you OK?" I said, "Yes." I opened my blouse and saw an incision on my chest. Through it, I became my own voyeur. I watched how my body was transforming. I saw some wings trapped in a cocoon. "Great, I can finally say good-bye to my flesh!" You know, *carne-vale*. [*A beat*] I did not fly immediately. I was holding my body in my hands like a traveling bag, waiting to depart so that I may leave what hurt me behind. [*A pause*] I don't know about you, but my body ached for too long … and now it has started to rise … like dough … [*Looking around,*] Where is that glass of water?

[*A glass of water descends theatrically from above.* SUN *pours water on top of her head. She smiles.*]

I am hungry. [*Sniffs*] Coriander? Basil? Paprika? Chicken paprika? Every now and then, I give myself permission to travel, to see fingers dirtied because of spices, to see them turning into a different hue than my skin. I reach for some strands of my hair that are coming down my face [because I did not tie it properly], and, in doing that simple gesture, I smell that paprika and think of old times when spices traveled on roads and people *stopped* to listen to stories. I put a finger in my mouth and that makes me travel back in time when I used to help grandma make *dulceață de nuci verzi* and our hands were yellowish-green on account of iodine. And the smell … ! The smell of a *woman*! [*She starts to leave the stage and makes a sign to* RENAISSANCE *to follow*] Try it alone. Close the drapes. It is time.

[*The photo returns, this time it is animated so that the cuts made by the scissors are felt and we see a montage of women starting to do gender-based roles, in the house, at the park, in line at a grocery store, in a delivery room, etc. They all start to run. They enter the tea garden in Istanbul panting. Stillness. The camera pans out to let us enjoy gorgeous views, of the landscape, of women. Music. Then, explosive laughter.*]

END OF CHOREOPOEM

About the Photo

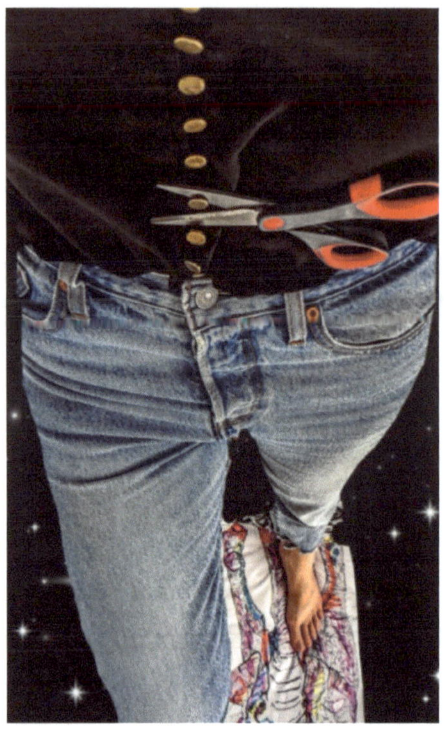

In the 1960s, Henri Matisse created cut-outs as a way of artistic freedom. He wanted to know how far he could stretch his inquiry into an artistic expression that, back then, was pretty standard, that is, it involved paintbrushes, a canvas, and an artist's imagination. These cut-outs will be revolutionary, thus opening the medium to explore uncharted territories. My piece was done as a consequence of my curiosity to feel the cold blades of the scissors between my fingers and then allow that to be transferred onto my upper body. I wanted to see if, when a pair of scissors does not cut, but it could, how that may feel. Imagine you are scheduled for a flu shot. You may be fearful or not of needles. But your brain could definitely make it better or worse for you. If opened, our bodies will change their physical and emotional maps on any given second. That is how complex we really are! We are made out of roughly 30 trillion cells! And that's not even it. We are so much more. During the longest year of our lives that started mid-March in the US (but sooner in China and, if we are honest, here, too), a year that is not yet over because the pandemic is not, as an artist, a woman, a mother, a sister, a partner, an educator, I had to face all my demons, clean up my own mess, and attempt to move on. Everything that I create is not in the name of a political statement, but to secure my happiness. If I am happy, then I am free. I have been waiting my entire life to be free.

Fictional Journeys

Amy Le

"Tree"[1]

Ommo and I walk down the row of vendors in zone two of the camp with Thủy-Tiên wanting to hold his hand not mine. On either side, there are people selling various items in the stands. There is even a café under a blue tarp and a small restaurant nearby. Some of the strangers stare at us inquisitively, while others, judgmentally. I am paranoid they will spread rumors that I am sleeping with this man to get special treatment. I pause to smell the coffee beans and close my eyes to enjoy the aroma.

"Would you like a cup of coffee?" asks Ommo.

"No," I lie.

"Sit. I want coffee." Ommo orders two cups of coffee and warm tea for my daughter. "Why do you hate me so much?"

"I no hate—"

"I have been trying to make things right with you ever since we met and I apologized for hitting your boat mates. I was following Abu's orders. I played music for you—"

"Not for me, for—"

"No, for you, Snow, and I brought you sapodilla fruit from my mother's tree. I pulled favors to get your family into a barrack and got your application processed with priority."

I am stunned and speechless. He is exasperated with me. He throws his hand in the air as if to say "I give up" and rubs his palms on his knees.

Our drinks arrive. I take a sip of the hot coffee. If only every moment in life is like the first sip. "Thank you."

Ommo relaxes his shoulders. "You are welcome."

"I need to find my nephew."

"I will help."

"I wish to see my friends too. Do you know where they are?" I ask.

---

1   Excerpt from the original novel, *Snow in Vietnam*, Mercury West Publishing, 2019.

He takes out a pen and small pad of paper from his shirt pocket. "Write down their names and I will find them." I write down Hồng-Mai's and Tùng's name, as well as Sơn's and Minh-Tú's. "I need more than their first names. I need surnames. There are thousands of people here with the same names."

"I sorry. I have only first names. Maybe you check names of everyone arrive to Galang on same day as me."

Ommo sighs. "I will see what I can do." He abruptly whips his head around and addresses curtly the two women working the coffee stand. He says something to them in Indonesian and they stop speaking to each other.

"They are spreading rumors about us," he says.

"What they say?" I am upset.

"They think we are lovers." He winks at me.

I blush and divert my attention to Thủy-Tiên. We spend the next ten minutes enjoying our drinks and talking about my daughter's health and what heart surgery would mean for her. Ommo escorts us back to the barrack via a longer route. He walks leisurely and is in no hurry to get out of the mud and rain. We arrive at my barrack the same time as Tree.

I lunge for my nephew to grab his ear. I am furious he has been out all night and caused us to miss the opportunity to go to Sweden. Before I can yell at him, he collapses to the ground.

Ommo carries Tree into our room and places him on my mattress. "He is burning up."

I grab a towel and run down the stairs to the drum of fresh rainwater. With the towel soaked in cold water, I run back and apply it to Tree's face and neck. "We need a doctor and medicine."

Thủy-Tiên, Mai, Khải, and the twins stand by helplessly.

"There are none that will come to you," Ommo says. "If he had a minor illness and the strength to stand in line, he can visit the Red Cross tent for treatment."

"He cannot die." I am terrified. "So many people get bury here and their site have no sign. No dignity for them."

"He will not die." Ommo places a reassuring hand on mine.

Tree is conscious and shivers. "I am cold."

I wipe the moisture off his face. I do not know if the beads are from his sweat or the rain.

Ommo offers a diagnosis. "It is possible he was bitten by a snake in the forest or ate something bad." Tree writhes in discomfort and it reminds me of Tuấn, when he had pinworms in his body. "Try to keep him cool and as comfortable as possible. I have to report to work after my lunch break." Ommo reluctantly leaves our side with the promise to return later with medicine for Tree's fever.

***

My defiant nephew has been sick for over a month but he is getting stronger. Headaches and abdominal pains are frequent visitors, so is vomiting and diarrhea. Khải helps Tree downstairs whenever my nephew needs to throw up or have a bowel movement. Sometimes, they are not fast enough or Tree is not strong enough so Mai helps me clean up. I pray several times a day.

Dear Lord, in Your light I entrust You with our lives. Please Heavenly Father, wrap Your protective arms around Tree and place Your healing hands on him. Keep us safe from harm and deliver us to freedom. Please also bless the friends and families in our lives. In Thy holy name I pray, Amen.

I have learned that Tree has been infected with malaria. Sometimes his body will convulse and he passes out from exhaustion. I feed him water with a spoon to keep him hydrated and sleep next to him to try to keep him warm. All day and night I keep vigil and have no energy for myself. I give Tree the malaria pills that the Red Cross gave us. The pills bring back haunting memories of Mrs. Trần overdosing on chloroquine. My roommates are a blessing and help with Thủy-Tiên. They take her with them to the dining hall to eat and bring back food. They help her go to the bathroom and take her to the beach for bathing and distractions. The twins have become her older sisters and play with her. They cleverly take stones they find and scrape the edges on the cement to smooth the surface into round balls and shoot them like marbles. With the subsistence allowance from the UNHCR and through Ommo's kindness, I am able to buy two mosquito nets.

Ommo and I have become friends this past month. The twins and Thủy-Tiên adore him. He brings them a treat when he visits or plays marbles with them and talks to them like little adults. I want to trust him but my experience with Minh-Hoàng reminds me to never let my guard down. I want to love him but every man I try to love ends up gone from my life. Mai is smitten with him and says he looks like a movie star. Khải is not happy when Ommo visits, mainly out of jealousy, but he tolerates him, probably because Ommo is in a position to make life either comfortable or difficult.

"I have some news for you today," says Ommo. "Can we talk outside, the two of us?"

I leave Thủy-Tiên with the twins and Tree with Mai and Khải. We walk outside towards the church that the other refugees are erecting from supplies provided by humanitarian organizations. The sun shines brightly so we find a tree to sit down against.

"I have made contact with your four friends," Ommo says.

"That is wonderful. I want to see them," I say.

"I informed Sơn and Minh-Tú you were in barrack two and they will visit."

"Thank you. What about Tùng and his sister?"

"I do not have good news about Hồng-Mai. Last month she was raped while heading to the toilet. She cannot identify her assailant. It could have been a guard or a refugee at the camp. Her brother is quite distraught."

The shock of this news shakes my core. I can only imagine the pain and shame Hồng-Mai is going through and how alone she must feel. I burst into tears.

Ommo wraps his arms around me. "You need to go see them today. Her brother is beside himself with worry and cannot comfort her. She will not talk to him or let him touch her. She will not eat or bathe."

I give in to his comforting embrace. "Take me to her. We go now."

"The police are investigating the incident. I requested a caseworker and a legal officer—"

"Now, Ommo. We go now. I need to see her."

***

Hồng-Mai's face is barely recognizable. She lies on the clay floor in a trancelike state of mind. She is emaciated and smells bad. I suspect it has been a couple of weeks since she last bathed. She exhales. The foulness of her breath makes me cringe.

Tùng also looks lethargic. "I am weary of living." Tùng drops his head into his hands. "I am going insane here."

"Your sister needs you to help her get through this." I gently touch his hand. "We need to be strong for her and I will be strong for you."

"We do not want to suffer anymore." Tùng grabs hold of my hands and squeezes. His tight grip of desperation cuts off my circulation.

I notice my fingers turning red and try to extract them from his grip. "Everyone here is in their own tormented hellhole, but if you wait a little longer, you will find light again."

Tùng sobs. "There is too much darkness to find light." He leaves his bamboo hut to cry alone. Ommo exits to follow him and leaves me with Hồng-Mai.

I slowly caress Hồng-Mai's head. "We will get justice for you and destroy the man who did this to you. Do not be ashamed." I remove the strands of hair from her face. "You did not cause this. Let me be your strength, Hồng-Mai. Lean on me. You are not going through this alone. I am here with you. Do you understand me? We will take it one day at a time. Together." Hồng-Mai clings to me and cries uncontrollably. The tighter she squeezes, the tighter I squeeze back. "Be strong and persevere. Is that not what Buddha teaches you?" I rub her back and soothe her as if she were a child. "Negative thoughts will lead to more suffering. I will find some incense to burn. We will ask a monk or a nun to chant for you to purify your mind and meditate with you, so you can find enlightenment." I lift her face up so she can see mine. "Hồng-Mai, remember, it is wrong to take a life, so eradicate those poisonous ideas."

Hồng-Mai weeps louder. I hold her tight and rock her. Together we share her sorrow.

***

A week has passed. Tree's energy is rising to the peak of his recovery and he wants to go for a swim. I am comforted by his enthusiasm and appetite. Even Hồng-Mai appears to be healing although the emotional scar will always be with her. I help her bathe daily by wiping her down with a wet washcloth and scrub her scalp and hair with a bar of soap before rinsing it. Today, I leave Hồng-Mai for a couple hours to sit with my nephew on the beach and enjoy a bowl of rice and pâté while Thủy-Tiên slurps on her porridge.

"I am sorry for disrespecting you and ruining our chance of leaving here to go to Sweden," says Tree.

"All is forgiven. I understand how much you miss home. You are becoming a man and you were dealing with everything the best way you could. I have put a lot of pressure and demands on you and that is a heavy burden of responsibilities."

"I enjoy being helpful. It makes me feel worthy, but I miss my parents and my little brother."

"I strongly believe we will go to America one day," I say. "I hope we can sponsor them."

"Are you sure that is still what you want? I mean, you can have a life here."

"In the camp?"

Tree laughs. "No, I mean with Ommo. He likes you and you like him too but will not admit it."

"I hung my fishing net a long time ago, Tree. I do not want a man to complicate my life. You and Thủy-Tiên are my life now. You both come first."

"More refugees arrive every day and live in makeshift houses. It will be only a matter of time before they build a second camp and we take over this island. Ommo can take you away from all this."

"It is turning into a tent island for sure. There are rice bags and tarps hung everywhere for shade, and fishing line or rope to hang clothes. Ommo is a convenient solution but it would not be right to take advantage of him. And I am not in love with him."

"In time you can love him. He is a good man in the wrong uniform. He serves Indonesia but his heart serves you. I am sure of it."

I laugh. "Tree, you are a romantic. Come, we need to swim."

The three of us splash around in the water for the next hour to forget our problems. Thủy-Tiên finds a crawfish and wants to keep him as a pet. She is mad and pouts when I tell her no.

Sandra Soli

Year of the Probable Boom 1953: Fear of Fallout

We follow each other like young lemmings, past the giant dictionary and coat room that smells of fourth-grade sweat, to an interior hallway next to the janitor's closet. We crouch on the floor, heads to knees, for the drill. Mrs. Foster reads from the instruction manual in a clipped allegretto: *Now clasp your hands behind your head like this. Stay down until the All-Clear sounds.*

Tornado rehearsals emancipated us for nearly an hour each spring and fall, so useless that we never took them seriously. If it's your turn for a tornado wipeout, there is no getting out of it. But today even the giggliest of us were solemn-faced, twisting to peer at classmates from beneath skinned elbows. This time, we were practicing to stay alive in the event of an atomic attack, which the school board decided would occur not only soon, but during school hours.

The principal had issued a procedure for atomic bomb drills on the first Wednesday of each month: orderly and precise, no deviation acceptable. Maximum survival rates would be achieved, if not nation-wide, then at least at Jefferson Elementary. Protocol demanded that we be inspired to global service. Mr. Douglas stepped into our room during Geography to assure us that Jeffersonians would lead the country back to normalcy and peaceful coexistence in a fragile-but-ever-expanding world, though he never explained how we might expect to be called on by the President, or even our parents, to set things right.

Don't look, reminds Mrs. Foster, explaining flashblindness.

We must shield our eyes from the soundless puff of light that will grow to fill the sky. A glorious blossom of fire, she warns, like nothing we ever imagined, but for our country's sake and our own, we must not look. On the way home I search the clouds for suspicious shapes, squinting at the sun, daring it to explode.

Since the only atomic mushrooms any of us encountered were on "Movietone News," patriotic eagerness eventually shriveled. We returned to playing jacks at recess (girls), strutting on the sidewalk (boys), and from hunched hallway poses, rolling our eyes in tacit agreement that Mrs. Foster's visions of floral fire were a product of wishful thinking. Gossips and gum-spitters, marble-shooters with chalky pockets, we practiced for Doomsday in lumpy hallway rows that never achieved the efficiency our elders hoped for.

We studied *Weekly Reader* news, pictures of Hiroshima, maps of Bimini in the Marshall Islands, and Bikini Atoll, with its legacy of eye-popping swimsuits. Eniwetok was best. We could jump to that, double ropes. We made up rhymes. *Doom rhymes with tomb, and Soon a big boom—or Toast, Toast, she's burnt toast … .* The boys stayed on the opposite corner. *Mine is bigger than yours. No, it isn't. Yes, it is.* Scientists set the Doomsday Clock for two minutes before midnight. The evening news mentioned a rumor that Polynesian children were falling sick. Atomic snowfall. Had they been dumb enough to stick out their tongues to taste white rain? Why would a shampoo company expect us to rub that stuff on our heads? Images of wet hair, falling out in my hands, converged with pineapples and snow maidens from Paradise in neon dreams that would not wait for sleep, blinking on as I stepped into the shower or began a spelling test. E-N-I-W-E-T-O-K. Ticktock, ticktock. Tick. Tock.

Fallout shelter signs appeared around town and the stress level for adults intensified. They consulted with contractors after fliers appeared in screen doors with "unretouched" photos of an Asian dead body, unrecognizable but sufficiently horrifying. Many of these "atomic engineers" had previously been hardware store employees or *Encyclopedia Britannica* salesmen, but in 1953, they traveled among worried homeowners to offer counseling and free estimates for family backyard shelters.

These pitch men wore suits and Thom McAn shoes as they handed out brochures: WHAT TO DO IN CASE OF ATOMIC ATTACK and SUPPLIES FOR YOUR SHELTER. There were ethical considerations too. People who purchased a shelter now had to draw up a list of friends and relatives allowed in when the most desperate of times arrived. The list could not exceed the number specified in a booklet distributed with solemnity: MAXIMUM OCCUPANCY LEVELS FOR YOUR SHELTER.

Reading the thing made a number of buyers feel guilty enough to step up to the next price bracket and a slightly larger hole in the ground, one that would include even Uncle Wally with bad breath. Wally could always sit facing the shelves of canned food, and what's an extra can of peaches when it's family?

Our next-door neighbor explained how everything would work. Mother suggested I could hold my opinions to myself and mind my Ps and Qs. Something big was due down the pike and at least we were on Harvey Thompson's APPROVED list, by virtue of us being on our own. Mom was a cute divorcée with great legs, so in an emergency she wouldn't be a bad sight backed up against shelves of peaches, either.

Not that Mr. Thompson had a perverted bone in his body. Besides, he bought one of the top models in the catalog: space for eight with supply cabinets, a fold-out table, and four water containers approved for 90 days' consumption without possibility of contamination. This baby even featured a built-in bookshelf to keep us schooled and entertained until we could safely return to the surface world. Everything had been fully tested in somebody's laboratory. We were sure to survive. Our only problem would be deciding when it would be safe to come above ground to a transformed universe. Mr. Thompson spent weeks on downwind calculations, finally pitching his notebook with a flourish.

"Hell, those government boys know what they're talking about. They'll come on the radio and let us know when it's time." He was over putting a thermostat in my mother's oven. It was always something, anything for the excuse to show off scientific theories carefully archived in that red spiral book.

"This here's important, you know. All the procedures. You girls don't worry about a thing." My mother listened with interest and thanked him for coming right over. Until the nuclear zap we at least had a stove that wouldn't burn those wonderful new frozen dinners. Peas tasted like little pasture rocks but were such a beautiful green. Miracles were possible in this era of modern convenience, even serving dinner in foil pans and getting on the approved list for a below-ground shelter that could withstand a blast as close as 80 miles. Parents were secure among the luxuries of TV trays, Swedish meatballs, peas that tasted like gravel, and instant potatoes. Kids were safe at school with monthly drills and gum-spitting contests. Neighbors cared for us and practiced putting on gas masks. Life was undependable, but good.

Mr. Thompson visited his shelter monthly to comply with warranty rules, double-checking shelves and renewing the water supply. On our screened-in front porch, I read horror comics that I had swiped from Gary down the street, sneaking looks over the top of the page as Mr. T. unlocked the padlock with a key he kept around his neck. I would immediately lose track of mutant tomato people breaking into mausoleums for the bigger drama of Harvey Thompson heading down into the murky dark, an act that would mean the difference between life and death for people on his list. My mother kept smiling at him.

I didn't think it mattered if we kept our place in line next door, but to her this was paramount. It never once occurred to me, little smarty bird-legs with an assy attitude, that all this was for my sake. Nothing happened. We gathered to watch Betty Furness sell refrigerators and Jack Benny play violin on the first television set in the neighborhood at Nicky Green's house; that is, until I gave him two purple Easter chicks that grew into hens, following me around the apartment. My mother trained them to a kitty litter box but said they weren't lovable anymore. Nick had my chickens less than a week before something got into the pen and killed the lot, his *farm* chickens and two little darlings that had perched at my feet while I read to them from Nancy Drew.

We waited out the atomic blast. Because of the chicken thing, I didn't speak to Nicky for two months and had to give up the television birth of Lucy Ricardo's baby for radio offerings. I hardly moved on Sunday afternoons, mother running the sweeper and me turning up the sound to hear Lamont Cranston's erotic baritone. *Who knows what evil lurks in the hearts of men? The Shadow knows.* Radio had its merits. I counted box tops to send for free stuff like Stamp Kits from Around the World, and heard Bert Parks play "Stop the Music!" with contestants whose hair wasn't falling out.

But still no bingo. Mother paid the rent on time and I called her every day after school to let her know I made it home okay and now would head for the library, where among other delights I studied sex in the stacks (Frank Yerby novels and the medical dictionary, in case you were wondering).

After two years it became evident even to Mr. Thompson that we weren't going to come under attack any time soon. He hauled his cans of green beans and peaches back into the house, prepared a garden adjacent to the bomb shelter, and moved his son Ellsworth out there to live. Ellsworth was seventeen. We all knew he was banished because his father couldn't stand him, even though Ellsworth was his own kid.

Ellsworth liked it, hung a sign over the door saying, "Frenchman Flat II." He invited his friends, not skinny-legged next-door neighbors. I sat in the grass painting my toenails and wishing he'd notice. I imagined going down the stairs into his private cave, that secret male place, the smell of Camel cigarettes and posters on the wall that you couldn't see without a flashlight. Oh, yeah, there was electricity. I guess Ellsworth didn't need the flashlight.

None of this was true, probably, but I thought about it a lot. Ellsworth was the only person I knew who lived in a bomb shelter and entered his own house just long enough to eat. Figured all that isolation would eventually get him, and about that one thing, I was right. Saying he had to have room to move around in, Ellsworth ran away to Australia and sired sons one after the other by an assortment of interesting women. Mother, who never gave up believing in the atomic age, imagined a slight skin problem and visited a dermatologist in Tulsa, who prescribed weekly radiation treatments. After her sessions I shivered to watch her skin turn shiny and red, smooth as the polished apple in Snow White. That was after Ellsworth stopped writing home and poor Mr. T. quit coming over because he had nothing to hope for, not even catastrophe.

Explosions eventually did burst into my life, none of them like flowers. I finally decided Harvey Thompson was a brave man. I'd like to tell him I'm sorry for being a brat and it was good to be on his list. Approved.

Alexander Weinstein

Sanctuary[1]

Early Visitations

The first to stumble across the new lifeforms weren't NASA scientists or marine biologists, but a group of teenage gamers who posted their findings on GameShare. Their retweeted video arrived on our phones looking like classic clickbait but soon circulated every social media feed until even news stations were replaying the clip. We watched the recording and listened to the young boys' voices.

Any of you see that?

See what?

Right side, past the cliff.

Got it. All zombies dead.

No, past the zombies—like on the side of the cliff.

Whoa. What the hell?

I don't know.

Is that part of the game?

I don't think so.

Whoa!

Newscasters enlarged the image, and there it was, climbing through a rip in the fabric of the immersive game, as real as any living creature we'd ever seen. Its mouth snapped at the air and the pixels around its body flickered with the prism of deep programming glitches. Yet, in interview after interview, programmers reported this wasn't an elaborate Easter egg, nor a technological prank or some cybernetic stunt. "We don't know what that *thing* is," they said, looking pale. It sure didn't seem like they were lying.

Our own first encounters were in online offices, eClassrooms, and immersive yoga studios. "Breathe in," our teacher instructed. We inhaled, stretched our arms above our heads, listened to our avatar yogini. Indian fusion played in our ears, the sound of a sitar and tabla

---

1   This story first appeared in *The Adroit Journal*, issue 31.

layered over a slow ebbing bass line, and we lowered ourselves onto the bamboo floor in the golden light of morning. Sunlight broke through the muslin curtains and something shimmered in the air, creating small waves in our vision. We readjusted our headsets, wondering if our system was glitching, but the console seemed fine.

"Stretch into downward dog," our teacher said, but we kept our eyes on the place where the room was pushing outward until, as though the studio was made of fabric, the air tore open and we gazed into the inky starriness speckled with planets, wondering if this was enlightenment.

Then an enormous green leg with small hairs and a chitinous shell pushed through the rip and stepped onto the bamboo floor. Another leg appeared, followed by a colossal mantis head which tore through the top of the gash. The creature's eyes were the size of dinner plates, and its segmented mouth emitted a series of high-pitched clicks as it examined us. We fled from our yoga mats and ran toward the studio doors. Then, remembering we were online, we pulled the headsets from our eyes, and stood terrified in the safety of our home offices, our IR consoles whirring quietly as we recalled how the creature had looked. It was almost as if *it* had been the frightened one.

Speculations

We assumed the creatures were nothing more than well-developed pranks, the kind of spam dreamed up by the technologically savvy to wreak havoc on our immersive worlds. And soon we received emailed apologies from our content providers confirming our assumptions. Everything, they assured us, was under control; the best of their IT departments were handling the glitches. For a couple of hours, a day at most, our movie streaming services, online games, and immersive environments would be shut down so they could find the virus and deprogram the bugs which were appearing across our landscapes.

Those of us attempting to log into meditation classes found SITE NOT AVAILABLE illuminated against the inside of our goggles. Our children, who'd paid for upgrades of cars and weapons, discovered blank screens. College classrooms were gone, as were our day-care centers and gyms. There was nothing but the darkness of our goggles and the blinking lights of our consoles.

That evening we listened to public statements from the CEOs of major immersive corporations. They were still establishing attribution for the massive cyberattack, which as far as anyone could see had compromised every platform across the globe. As they tackled this major breach, we were not to reconnect or attempt to delete the bugs on our own. They'd find the hackers, they promised us.

But when our systems remained inoperative for over twenty-four hours, we turned to the blog posts emerging from Silicon Valley. The companies, it was rumored, had hired white hat hackers, who'd reached out to black hat hackers, who'd turned to the most nefarious code-crackers on the Dark Web for help. What was going on, we wanted to know. When, we demanded, would our access be restored? And what were those creatures? RATs, worms, Trojan horses? Were the mantids a zombie army of bots, infecting our machines and using our consoles to do some evil hacker's bidding? Yet none of our guesses rang true. For if the glitches had been ransomware, where were the requests for our money? And if they were adware, why hadn't the creatures tried to sell us anything?

The Blossom Files

It was then that the black hat hacker known as Scott Blossom appeared. He leaked the internal memos of the largest corporations and shared the data mining done by their hired code-crackers. The companies, he told us, had gotten so desperate they'd reached out to third-world scammers, bitcoin miners, and Dark Net thieves. All the while, their meticulously designed landscapes were being ruined by the presence of the insects. Here were images of giant grasshoppers amid Sega's Indy 500 games and enormous praying mantises materializing in immersive gyms. And then, Blossom revealed the truth: the bugs were extraterrestrials trapped within our immersive worlds—the most real thing in our unreal realities—and though the insects could interact with our coding, there were no traces of them in the programming, no data whatsoever.

The thrill of extraterrestrials filled us with nervous excitement. What planet had they come from? Were we in life-threatening danger? What intergalactic message would they deliver? Amid our questions hung a shadow of guilt. We recalled the conference rooms where we'd hurled office chairs at them, the online birthday parties where we'd grabbed our children, the college campuses where the creatures had clattered into the classroom, clumsy as horses. We'd flung scalding coffee at them and tried to cripple the bugs with our yoga mats, though they'd done nothing more than place their front legs on our conference tables, their large antennae frantically flickering as they suffered the digital objects we'd hurled at them.

We wanted to see the creatures again. Our providers had no right to deny us service. This miraculous event wasn't their discovery to keep. We flooded phone lines and filled in-boxes. The most politically active surrounded corporate offices with signs and bullhorns. And finally, the CEO of a Buddhist meditation module relented. He sent out an email extolling the ethos of an open web and reopened his immersive monastery. Soon other start-ups followed, then gaming companies, then Google, then Apple, and finally our connections flickered back to life and protesters returned home to place their goggles over their eyes.

The wounded creatures were still cowering in our restaurants and conference rooms, and we approached them cautiously. Wasn't it true that after mating female mantises ripped the heads off their partners? Couldn't they crush spines as easily as they did exoskeletons? We worried they'd seize us in their front legs and stare at us with their compound eyes before tearing off our heads. But the creatures were no more dangerous than butterflies trapped in a glass, and as we gathered around them, they only stared at us, as if trying to determine whether we meant them harm.

Sanctuary

Tasha Cozhani's piece first appeared in *The New York Times* and later in our social media feeds, expanded upon thereafter by a thousand bloggers, corroborated by hundreds of scientists, and finally, voiced by one or two of our politicians. Cozhani was a professor of entomology at Cornell's immersive campus. She studied grasshoppers, aphids, and mantises, understood their migratory patterns, knew how their congregations acted when threatened. These creatures, she wrote, weren't the same as our own insects, though there were clear parallels. For one, instinctual reactions when traumatized. She referenced heart rates, swollen abdomens, ovipositor dysfunction. Immersive reality, Cozhani speculated, had been the intergalactic architecture through which we'd extended our communication tower, and our signal had been picked up. These creatures weren't coming to attack us, nor to invade or destroy; they were arriving at our invitation to seek sanctuary.

A group of entomologists from Prague corroborated Cozhani's theory, pointing to lacerations on wings, broken tibial spines, and cracked raptorial appendages. Not only were the insects highly intelligent but their intent was in no way malevolent. The creatures had been mistreated, they said, and seemed to have escaped from their own world to seek refuge in ours. They weren't hostile, nor were they the Antichrist as our religious leaders claimed; they'd simply arrived to our shores seeking something better.

"Delusional" was what AM talk-show hosts called Cozhani's theories. These insects were highly dangerous—keepers of decay, squirming with neurotoxins and poisonous mandibles. Their bodies hid viruses that would corrupt our landscapes. An invasion of bugs destroying immersive reality was simply the start of a larger migration.

World leaders were in a panic. Already, more insects were appearing upon our virtual shores, floating through torn portals like boats emerging from fog. But what was their message? They arrived with neither greetings of peace nor threats of war. They merely stood in our IR environments, their heads reaching the ceilings of our offices, staring at us with their silvery eyes as they chirped indecipherably. And soon we found ourselves in one of two camps: those who'd fed ants sugar crystals and watched them build tunnels in glass terrariums, and those who'd held magnifying glasses over their backs to watch them curl and incinerate under the sun's concentrated ray.

A Victoria's Secret store closed when two massive grasshoppers appeared, pushing racks aside as they clattered through the aisles. A Carnival cruise had to refund payments when one of their immersive ocean liners became home to a dozen escaping mantids. A group of toddlers were terrified by a gigantic bleeding grasshopper that had appeared in their day-care center. And, finally, an Alabama county clerk named Frannie Sheffield had an anxiety attack when a praying mantis appeared at the office's immersive picnic. Her round face was broadcast on all the channels as she lay in her hospital bed, voicing the request of an increasing number of Americans. "Squash them," she said to the cameras.

It was a phrase soon chanted by others. They emerged in our communities with signs and T-shirts. "Squash them," they chanted outside the corporate offices of our immersive-content providers. The Fraternal Order of Police issued a unified statement condemning the interstellar creatures. Religious leaders quoted Bible verses about pestilence, infestations, and blights, and conservative talk show hosts gave inaccurate history lessons on the boll weevil. "What we need to do," a Georgia senator said, "is put up a firewall so powerful it'll roast those crickets." And finally, an immersive-home owner in Pendleton, Oregon, loaded a virtual shotgun and opened fire on the mantis that had emerged on the front lawn of his online home. We saw his face on the news stations the next day, the carcass of the creature behind him. "If the corporations aren't going to keep us safe," he said, "it's up to us to defend ourselves."

The Official Response

The president appeared on our smartphones, and we took off our IR goggles and gathered to hear him. America, he announced, was under attack. The immersives had precipitated a national crisis that threatened our cities, our homes, and our way of life. Despite the claims of liberal media outlets, these creatures weren't docile or here in peace. These bugs were intergalactic predators opening the doors of our immersive worlds in advance of even more horrific insects, and their appearance in our digital world was nothing more than a prelude to their invasion of our real one.

And yet, the president's fears didn't match reality. No giant mantises were emerging in our actual midst, nor were the creatures a danger to our children. They poked their heads peacefully into our infants' *Sesame Street* tutorials. Alongside Big Bird there now squatted an enormous grasshopper, and our immersive dance studios were becoming home to injured arrivals who wanted nothing more than food and water.

But the president had issued his Executive Order. A new immersive military was being formed. Online forces were ready to stop any creatures who attempted to crash our virtual borders. He praised the Pendleton shooter and urged our teenagers to turn their tanks from the war-torn landscapes of their video games toward the horizons which were dotted with insects. Blast the creatures with mortar shots, he said; use whatever resources you have to fight the aliens online. Then, facing the camera, he spoke the words we'd hoped never to hear.

"We are at war."

The First Days of War

When we logged back on, we found our offices and universities swarming with white trucks and avatars in hazmat suits wrangling insects into refrigerated HGVs. A large van screeched to a halt in front of our yoga class and armed soldiers descended upon the mantis with projectile nets. The creature's thin antennae beat against the mesh, and it looked at us with its large black eyes. It raised its wings, frantically opening and closing them against the nets until we heard something crack.

"*Stop!*" we yelled. But the men, being men, didn't listen. They bashed us with nightsticks and corralled us into corners. They shot the creature with tranquilizers and pulled it across the pavement into their trucks. We stood on the stained bamboo floor, watching the vans disappear into some Dark Web site where we couldn't follow. None of us felt like meditating anymore.

How many of them died in those early days, no one knows for sure. We demanded to know where the insects were being taken, but the president remained silent. Scott Blossom, who'd sought political asylum in Norway, leaked a video of cramped cages in an immersive detention center, the creatures mashed together within the wire pens as our president waged his war against the cosmos.

A group of black hat hackers arose in rebellion, programming temporary firewalls of safety which the government frantically sought to crash. The revolutionaries appeared on our screens with insect masks and a video of the enormous mantises they'd kept sheltered from the roaming feds. "We're creating a worldwide network of sanctuary sites," they announced. They spoke of encrypted warehouses hidden deep within the inner cities of our children's sandbox games, and of global protectorates scattered across the mountaintops of our skiing modules. It was up to us—hackers and everyday citizens—to hide and protect the creatures.

Those of us who'd never played video games, now lowered our goggles and sat with our ears cradled in headsets as we fought our government, faced firing squads, and respawned to fight again. Among the new heroes were shop owners and schoolteachers, pastors and firemen, mothers and fathers who hid grasshoppers in the basements of their online homes and offered sanctuary within immersive churches and monasteries.

In response, we were bombarded by more invective from the White House, praising the gamers who were amassing insect casualties, and extolling the virtues of the president's militiamen who were squashing the intruders online. As for the traitors who would protect them, the president announced he was sending real troops to kick in the doors of the Silicon Valley offices that housed the black hat anarchists. His hackers were already breaking through our firewalls; they were coming for our sanctuary sites.

We attempted to herd the creatures back through the virtual rifts, but like crickets jumping away from an open door they refused to leave, resisting as if fighting death itself. In the end, we watched them turn instead toward the open borders of our immersive worlds, where they cocked their heads, listening to the sound of the approaching tanks.

Intergalactic Songs

It was then that the creatures began to sing. The mantises, whose legs our doctors had mended, lifted their wings and rubbed them together, and their melodies rose above the gunfire with the sound of crickets on a summer evening. Their music reverberated across the rooftops of our blasted landscapes and set meditation bowls ringing, filling our bodies with a soft vibration that tasted like honey to our eardrums.

For a moment, we were awestruck by the beauty of their songs, which sounded almost like prayer. The citizens' brigades stopped marching, the dark-hearted gamers lowered their machine guns, and the tank operators idled in their war machines. Even those who at this late stage were still attempting to ignore the war and go shopping, paused and listened. The songs were beautiful, and for a moment we felt like children drawn to the glow of fireflies. The creatures' stridulations echoed from our sanctuary sites, a wave of exquisite music that was also a homing beacon to their hiding places. We tried to silence the creatures, but they just looked at us with their compound eyes and continued their melodies. Then, just as quickly as it had arisen, the spell was broken. The military trucks began to move again, the citizens began to march, the gunmen raised their controllers, and we finally understood a truth. Our visitors didn't need to destroy us—we were doing that ourselves—and the distance they'd traveled was far less than the gulf between us and our neighbors now. Had we had more time, perhaps we could have learned their languages, translated their songs, understood the reasons they were here. But the tanks were already arriving. So, we lifted our controllers and faced our fellow humans.

Nonfictional Hybrids

Alina Stefanescu

Forbidden[1]

1.

As the child of Eastern bloc defectors in Alabama, I grew up forbidden. True things grew inside the mother tongue that kept the heart secret. I blame my parents for my fascination with walls, fences, boundaries, barriers. I blame the sky for beguiling me. I blame language for carrying oceans.

2.

It is May, the second month of pandemic; the book in progress, side-lined by childcare. Time coils, crackles, loosens: I am torn between restlessness and the reckless loneliness of being trapped for months in a house with three children. My solution is simple: leave, run, escape by packing kids into the car and roaming backroads, our eyes peeled for meadows, space to roam outside the choir of sirens arriving and departing the three hospitals near our house.

Forty miles outside the city, a locked green metal gate appears, a road behind it winding towards hills. I tell the children this is IT. I park along the edge of a ditch.

The son notices the sign says NO TRESPASSING. He misunderstands the invitation.

"There is nothing *forbidding* here," I assure him, as an ordinary yellow butterfly settles on the gate, two long metal beams shaped like wings on a hinge with a side padlock. It is inviting. It is idyllic. It is the middle of nowhere: what a map calls Chalkville.

I have more to say but I keep the other things to myself. I turn the word *bucolic* on my tongue but do not offer it to the children. I keep *bucolic* quiet, preserving its connotations from their curiosity.

---

1   A version of this essay appeared on the author's personal website, at
    www.alinastefanescuwriter.com/blog/2021/5/28/forbidden

I save this word for a poem I haven't written. The poem is always there, simmering beneath the surface. At this point I care more about the word than the clamor of three children who make buzzing sounds in the absence of bees.

Look, I have done worse than what we are doing, I tell myself as we scale the gate, throw our legs over the top, drop our backpacks to the ground in different pitches of plunk.

The sun lengthens our shadows. The sun sprawls across shrubs like a mother at the beach who silences the world by unimagining its existence.

We walk past a paved driveway lined by trees, soaked in fresh chirps, a tiny creek dawdling to our left.

"It's not even a real creek!" the youngest announces, "it is a *tod-dler* creek." (She is the proud older cousin of a toddler.)

To the left, the son identifies a patch of cultivated daffodils— *definitely planted*, he confirms, *not wild*. Brown hair crawls over his shoulders like uncombed snakes. His hair is a separate wilding.

"This place had an official gardener on staff at some point," he says. He can tell from the layout.

The unreal creek toddles along with us for ten minutes, rounding a curve, passing a monstrous patch of kudzu.

Suddenly, a silhouette of a steeple appears in a vague forward, also known as the future, and it rubs against the past, rubs against that *once* when the middle daughter smelled a rotting rat beneath the porch. Now her eyes narrow. The middle daughter expresses concern about the vast kudzu kingdom—its hollows and hills, the shape and dull rolling—clearly *haunted*. She has a *strange feeling* about this place which strikes me as hopeful; hope being the condition of having and holding strange feelings close to our hearts.

When she lowers her voice to a whisper, I follow suit. "Micah is being exemplary," I whisper, stunned by how the change in volume changes the hue of the green things. This feels appropriate, the awe-filled tone correct when addressing a kudzu patch. It is respectful.

"But you are confusing *awe* with *foreboding*," my son corrects. He is very articulate and a frisbee of meaningfulness at odd moments. He is not the voice of reason, though he resembles this voice from a bird's nest.

"No," I insist. "This is the Church of Wandering; and there is the steeple. Every stop along the way may be part of the passion or else a tussock where a donkey paused to eat clover as a god thought his cross-thoughts. Surely we are monks in this."

I consider what it means to be a monk in an unforbidding place as we pass around a water bottle and start walking again. I resist the temptation to draw an analogy between sharing bottled water and drinking from the same chalice which might contain the blood of a man who is no longer alive. I maintain a relation to abstraction: *we are monkish.*

3.

We approach the ruins of a stone chapel with a hole carved by a wrecking ball in the front. "Something massive must have been removed," I say.

The son suspects it was a big old bell: a *bell-tower with an open wound.*

The urge to write slams into me like a train.

The kids want to keep going. One has a caterpillar on her shoe.

"But we are monks," I say, "this is our discipline—to bring all possible attention to bear on that gape-mouth wound." Life is a form of poetry, and poetry is a form of discipline, namely, the focus and attention of one who wants to be raptured. The methodology is to see what lies before us with the lover's insatiable eyes, the gaze that can't touch or taste in moderation.

The son makes disgusted noises.

I tell them to go ahead and ramble without me.

A purple flower lifts her anonymous face from a crack in the pavement. There is this *breeze*, I think, which is not quite a wind.

"What is Mom doing?" the son groans.

"She is staring at that hole with all her mightiness!" the youngest declares.

"Oh, look at that vine climbing through the window's eyeball," the middle daughter warns—"Oh this place is for sure haunted by horrors happening to children. It's like a tinfoil pinwheel."

Her simile disarms me. A good simile is a light that reveals without sterilizing the room for surgery. It is visible—it offers a tactile picture, its plastic tinfoil physicality embodying fear—not the abstraction but the cheap kitsch of its connotations clinging to what should be fun.

And isn't it funny how so much of what should be fun in childhood is actually terrifying?

I want to come back to the hole in the wall or the wound in the bell-tower, specifically, the location of this wound over the larynx of the bell-tower's throat. Is a bell-tower without a bell still a bell-tower?

When the son expresses hunger, I groan. The burden of childcare: entirely mine during pandemic. A childless female friend celebrates the extra time at home: "I'm going to finish my book," she announces. My husband has taken over my study to work from home.

I am somewhere between a steeple and a simile, thinking about mothering and losing your voice in winter and whether bells are like children who have disappeared behind the tall grass growing over the tennis courts. Whether children are closer to bells than missing balls. Only when faced with the weed-smothered tennis courts do I begin to wonder where we are. Why the tennis court nets are doused in vines. Why the children are hesitant. And I think about James Longenbach, who said a poem's power comes from its ability to resist its conclusions while being pulled toward them. I think about what it means to be haunted or remembered—and why the middle child is the one who keeps mentioning it. So much hinges on how we carve implication. Or what we want from the landscape.

4.

Crouched beside the tennis court, a long, ranch-style brick building waits, its edges thick with the white blooms of privet, the flowers open, sickly fragrant. The scent is too sweet, almost odious.

The children wander in circles, back back to the chapel whose entrance way is now visible, a hot pink, purple, orange and green clown face spray-painted across the wood front doors.

"Teens must have been here," my son says. He is a teen, and therefore an authority on teen-ness. He helped spray-paint a mural on a city wall last year under quasi-legal circumstances.

Above the clown's fluorescent leer, an engraved stone plaque makes its claim: *Thy word is a lamp unto my feet.*

"It doesn't make sense," the youngest says, "unless this was a night-night church and people needed night-lights to find it?"

The night-night church with a clown mouth and a wound in the bell-tower's throat.

There is another brick building across an empty parking lot. There is a pink flowering dogwood holding an umbrella over the shoulders of a cairn. There is no one here except us and the paint-tracks of teens and the scandal of empty buildings you can't see from the road.

Micah runs her eyes over the terrain. She reminds us that something *awful* was done here. She can sense it in her tummy like that time she ate too many roses off the brick wall and had to go to the doctor who said *parents should know better than to let kids eat roses.*

The middle child has carried this guilt for years: "You told me not to eat roses, Mom, but you never told the doctor that you told me."

I remember the doctor was pregnant, tired, probably not even listening.

I ask my daughter to let that go, just drop it in the Church of Wandering's invisible confessional where all is forgiven but not forgotten—all is important, luminous, but also one single impression. Not the whole story.

This, too, is a discipline. I have learned to give joy my full attention from failure, particularly, my inability to find joy in home decorating, in settling, in using the scripts shared by friends for recipes, good workouts, affirmations, crunches. As a child, I was the joyfullest melanchole in Tuscaloosa County. Now I am mothering its worried expressions.

My son rolls his acorn-eyes as I sit on the last moment this rock could be called a step and open my notebook.

"What happened to wandering?" he asks.

His voice fades. I wander inside. I wander off in my mind.

"You can still eat violets," I tell the children. Violets are packed with vitamin C and stardust. I gesture towards a clump nearby.

A purple clover actually resembles the instant before black hole swallows matter. I take notes. I confess. Here's what I know: it is easier to parse birds than to discuss how a face turns ominous or the way bricks change the tenor of nearby dahlias or the mist in his eyes when he kissed me. The not-blue of it.

The notebook carries the conversations no one wants to have with me. My commitment to the notebook—and to writing—includes a commitment to these conversations that raze me, that raised me, that keep razing and raising the roof. I am happy when writing these things which make the world in which no one talks about a little more tolerable.

The notebook is a secret closet where I go to resolve things.

The notebook is the stable where the horses I've invented by discipline wait for me to ride them.

"I'm really scared," the middle child says. Her voice is trembly, willow-like. She wants to go home and maybe come back with Daddy. There *could be teens hiding* in the buildings. No one knows where we are.

Where are we?

The wind lifts the hair round her face and I think if any of us can read the sky, it is this one—it is this child, the little limner. I give in.

5.

Two days later, we return with my husband, official Daddy, paterfamilias, patriarch in residence.

"Since I'm driving," he says, "I need to know where we're going."

I say we don't know *exactly*. Near Chalkville. It's a place that existed with a steeple and a creek and tennis courts. Someone may have stolen the bell. It's behind a padlocked gate. It has thickets of rolling kudzu. It's a room in the world we want to know further. It's somewhere on this road if we keep going.

My husband merges, follow directions. When the metal gate appears, he pulls in and parks close to it. He takes his time collecting blankets, books, apples, extra water, a few beers.

A white truck passes slowly on the county road, looking official.

The son says we should probably hurry and jump the gate and get *in* there before someone stops us. Girls beat him to it. I follow.

As my husband locks the car behind him, the white truck reappears. The kids and I watch from the other side of the gate, safe within the Church of Wandering, as the white truck parks next to our car and an alarming white male emerges wearing a T-shirt tucked into his khakis.

"This is state property!" the man yells. "I am the city manager! It's a felony to trespass on state property!" He is walking and yelling in tandem, like sirens.

I remember sirens with no stitches between screams.

He waves his arms for me to come back: "Those kids have no business back there with Satan worshippers! There are Satanic people that go back there and I arrested two last week!"

My husband lowers the rim of his baseball cap until I can't see his face as he asks the city manager what this place was, or is, and why it belongs to the state.

The manager spits, his face flushed, camellia-like, two red dots on his cheeks resembling those of the church-going clown painted over the doors. "This was the home for Bad Girls! They kept misfitted daughters here!"

The middle daughter steps on my shoe, says she *knew it*. Didn't she warn us that *awful things happened* to kids here?

The son is as tall as the city manager, or so he is thinking, when he straightens his posture and notes: "It's hard to see the No Trespassing sign from the road. We must have missed it."

A blue truck honks three times in passing.

It is unfathomably sunny. I imagine thorns growing from teeth.

Something inside the city manager is rumbling, changing, struggling with something outside the city manager and it's impossible to name either thing—the most I can do is note the conflict.

"Look over there!" the manager points to the massive kudzu patch. "That is a crime! That was a Confederate graveyard until contractors used it as a dump for their clean-up."

The middle daughter says she knew it.

The manager asks what she knew.

The son says no one knows anything anyway we should just leave. This isn't fun anymore.

I tell the manager that we just wanted to have a family picnic, experiment with family values in a place we'd never explored.

The manager approaches me with his pointer finger directed at my chest: "I hereby declare myself *a constable*. As a constable, I have the capacity to haul you into jail and arrest you for a felony."

Constable. Capacity. Arrest. The last word isn't unfamiliar.

The littlest daughter tightens her grip, the sweat between our hands sealing us closer, a diluted glue. I want to comfort the kids and my man, but I'm mesmerized by the shape-shifting: how the manager has morphed into a constable without any strobe lights or magic smoke, only the power of a few words thrown from his mouth.

I hear myself saying *I have never met a constable* and *how nice to finally meet one*. What feels like magic may be the beard of a breeze my daughter construes as haunted. Or just a man using words to reinforce walls used to imprison young girls.

The manager's finger descends, the muscles in his neck soften, he says this whole place is haunted and we *don't know the half of it.*

My husband picks a tendril of honeysuckle vine and puts it on the dashboard as he repacks the car.

A brown chocolate labrador retriever appears from nowhere and nudges the dirt near the gate with his nose. The labrador lacks a collar. We don't know how long he's been here. Even the patch of white daffodils seems ominous—it must have been planted by the people who worked at the *home for bad girls.* The daffodils watched a graveyard get plowed over.

Since the manager's abracadabra, I wonder about signs, things I missed.

The middle daughter didn't miss any signs.

The littlest knows toddlers, the oldest knows teens, the middle one knows ghosts. Each has their angle of insight. I am here for the poem intended to house the word *bucolic.*

6.

In the car, it is quiet. I lay the honeysuckle over my left shoulder and let it slither across my arm like a feather boa or an honest snake. I let it settle into the snake it wants to be. "So where were we?"

I ask this knowing where we were is never far from where we are.

The map shows nothing. I search my phone for youth prisons and Chalkville. The words open it up. Known locally as the school for bad girls, the Alabama Training School for Girls housed "incorrigibles," "delinquents," or "waywards," most of whom were never formally charged with a crime. It was constructed in the 1930s to hold more than 150 youth with noncriminal violations. The Works Progress Administration helped dig the swimming pond and design the recreation areas for what would later be known as the Chalkville Detention Center.

In the ranch-style dorm building, there is a time-out room with a heavy metal door and tiny glass hole through which guards could view the girls placed in solitary confinement. Metal bunk beds lined the walls of the dormitory, and the heavy metal doors to the windowless sleeping rooms were locked at night.

We didn't get to explore this part. I learn about it by doing what a poet does when she finds a plant she can't describe—I looked for the root word, the etymology, the ways this plant had been used by others, the history.

"I knew it," the middle daughter says, her voice low to the floor.

7.

Other things I learn and share with the children: the 10,000-pound silver bell from the chapel was probably stolen by construction crews working to clean up the site after a level EF3 tornado with 150mph winds barreled through on January 2, 2012. Only eighteen girls and eight staff members remained in the school when the tornado hit during the night. As if by miracle, the dorm housing the residents and staff sustained the least damage. The cafeteria, school, and gym were completely leveled.

In 2001, forty-nine plaintiffs sued the state of Alabama for sexual misconduct involving the state Department of Youth Service's Chalkville Detention Center. The girls alleged that, between 1993 and 2001, they suffered sexual, mental, and physical abuse at the hands of the guards and staff.

The plaintiffs had been sentenced to serve time at Chalkville for shoplifting or drugs or skipping school or behaving in "unbecoming" ways. When their wealthier peers got expelled for similar behaviors, they went to elite private schools.

The line between good and bad in Alabama depends on income and access. None of the girls at Chalkville came from middle-class families. All were raised in poverty. In 2007, the state of Alabama settled the suit for $12.5 million. Each plaintiff received $255,102, from which they were required to first cover the trial expenses and attorney fees.

Things I don't share with the children: S. slept with a guard who promised her early release in return for her sexual cooperation. The guard then proceeded to do the same thing with S.'s room-mate. When S. rejected his advances, the guard added to her work detail and physical exercise regimen. S. said it was easier to just let him screw her— to lay there and watch her life leave its body in suspended animation. The school's superintendent did not believe her. According to media reports, the guard was *a great guy*, and *beloved*.

T. was surprised by the attention a shift supervisor paid her. At home, T. felt like an absence, a blank space, a mouth to feed. At Chalkville, T. was fascinating, worthy of a man's time and seduction. There were rumors of other girls he'd seduced at Chalkville. When T. realized she was pregnant, she sued the shift supervisor for paternity. Across the street in planned communities, other fathers watched football and wept for their teams between fists of beer and french fries.

8.

In a lecture on poetry, Jericho Brown said: "I am more interested in learning about why we'd be interested in immortality than I am in immortality itself." This is how I feel about poetry, about the notebooks, about what I want to taste, share, or keep separate. I am more interested in the source of the hunger than the fact of the hunger.

"Writing the poem is how we face the terror," Brown said. In this, "the poem mirrors the process of prayer." And the line-break is like doubt, waiting for the next line, holding faith in what follows from the word, the image, the thing which must be written. This is the thing you must write.

When the kids ask what the girls did that was so bad, I say it wasn't necessarily *bad* so much as forbidden.

The word *forbidden* comes from the English verb, *to forbid*, meaning to prohibit or command against. By the early thirteenth century, the expression "God forbid" is recorded. In Genesis 2:17, the Garden of Eden contains the "forbidden fruit."

There is no simple answer that doesn't violate human complexity. Nothing is fair but there are moments which teach us to kneel towards them. A story about surviving is complicated by what people expect from survivors, a redemption, an eschatology driven by guilt.

In this pandemic, I don't tell the kids other things I know about words—things I cannot translate into a mother:body.

We are complicit in your silences as much as our statements. See, I am the mother who withholds her own rape from the narrated life she offers her kids. I still cannot talk about it. The words are the metal gate I don't want to explore or open. It is forbidding, though not *forbidden*. It is something I cannot climb with any word that has ever touched me. It changed my life and yet I cannot help internalizing the belief that my sheer existence in a garden assumed the snake.

The patriarch's story wants my tears tangled in shame. The patriarchy includes allies who believe carceral systems can make us safe. What if the systems intended to save us are the sites of cyclic violence which ensure the continuance of the master's house?

Against the canticle of closed mouths, words can do difficult things. The city manager, for example, became a constable just by saying the magic words. But words cannot do everything. Not for women or girls. Words cannot remake a world broken by its cruelties. They cannot save our bodies. They cannot restore the past or redeem it: at best, words can reveal it.

This essay began with a barrier that felt formal, an inheritance of crossing borders. It progressed through a formal mode, namely wandering, that challenged the essays' linearity by invoking daydreams, unspent similes, strange bells. Now it ends in a space haunted by forbiddenness—a space whose history includes sexual abuse and cruelty at the hands of the carceral state. And silence: my inability to enact sexual violence on the page, my attempt to explain how a woman that jumps fences and risks arrest still cannot speak about rape. And this refusal is also poetry; my poetic "no" is complicated by a sense of duty to children and to our communities.

Rather than pretend to give a "fair account" of the horror that happened in Chalkville (an account I do not believe anyone outside the students is equipped to give), I must foreground the uncertainty, the fluctuating ideals of safety, the unknowable and known in our own adventure as a family—and my continuing silence in certain poems where *what I want to say* remains *what I refuse to be said by*.

I am here for the mystery. I am here for the power of words to break bread without breaking bodies. I mother my way through the institutions that fail children, the fences that hold us back from witness, the silences heavy in my own life and blood. I know so little over the long term, and the poem accepts this uncertainty, this complicity in erasure, this silence of bars.

The poem denies the innocence of culture in its construction of the criminal.

The poem permits the unknowingness which counters the prison industry, the profit made from criminalization of underprivileged bodies.

The patriarchy wants an answer, a clear delineation, an us vs. them which makes war and violence possible. But this is what the poem cannot give you.

I know a few languages, but I have no words for the shape injustice lays over recovery.

I know my middle daughter is the queen of foreboding. My son rarely combs his hair. My littlest daughter forbids her invisible pony from eating apples in the living room.

I hope we trust the *bad* girls more than we do the system that violates their humanity.

I hope we find a way to poem the most haunted places without shoving ghosts into boxes that suit our theories. I know the poem wants to touch what lies hidden behind a locked metal gate.

I know reality cannot fit the pastoral.

I know the word *bucolic* is still there, in my mouth, where it waits. It waits. Let us poem.

Let us wander.

Let us meet in the ruins of the belltower: the hole in its throat.

***

Sources

I have left the names of the Chalkville survivors as initials, though they are easily accessed in public records and news reports. Information about Chalkville Detention Center came from Kelly Kazek's reporting and photographs on https://www.al.com/. I am grateful to Val Walton's reporting for details on the lawsuit against the Alabama Department of Youth Services. Additional details and the stories of plaintiffs were sourced from Amy Singer's "Girls Sentenced to Abuse," *Marie Claire*, June 2002. Quotes from Jericho Brown come from "Faith in the Now: Some Notes on Poetry and Immortality", a lecture he gave at Breadloaf Writers Conference in the summer of 2019 (available at https://midd.hosted.panopto.com/Panopto/Pages/Viewer.aspx?id=e214d78c-dea8-439b-928b-aaac01599135).

N.S. Bala

The Heat of a Serpent's Hiss

I was never afraid of snakes as a small child. With their smooth bodies and bright colors, I was fascinated by their existence. I loved how they lived. I loved how they moved, so calm, cool and in control. Even the word "slither" evoked a sensuality that I thought matched the majesty of serpent's genus. Worms and bugs "wriggled" and "wiggled"—words that reflected their struggle for existence and basic survival. But "slither" did not imply energetic taxation. Instead, it evoked a sense of power that comes when one feels and moves with freedom and abandonment.

I always had a fascination with myths and folktales from around the world. But I was partial to the traditional myths and folktales from India. Some of my partiality came from the personal connections I had with those stories; connections that involved my grandmother telling these tales over the strong, bittersweet smell of her morning coffee. Others came from me reading collections of tales translated into English, out loud and often curled up against my grandmother, seated cross-legged on the floor where I would sneak sips of her delightful morning ritual between paragraphs. A common go-to for us were the collected stories known as *Panchatantrā*, a collection of folktales that spanned five volumes. Only later as an adult, I would slowly come to realize and reflect on the moral messages of these stories. But as a child, I only focused on how fantastical some of the stories were, where animals could talk and humans could transform into plants, animals, or even mundane household objects.

One of my favorite folktales was about the snake and the sage. The story went that once upon a time there was a deadly, poisonous snake that was terrorizing a village. Without warning, the snake would bite travelers that came in and out of the village, poison cows as they were grazing, and kill unsuspecting children who came into the little grove where he liked to sleep, looking for a stray ball. The villagers lived in constant fear of this serpent. One day, a sage came into the village, asking for alms and lodging. The villagers went to the sage and told him their problems with the deadly serpent. They begged him to help them.

The sage agreed, and the next day, set out towards the little grove where the snake lived. Seeing the sage approach, the snake asked him why he came to this area, knowing the dangers that it held. The sage replied that he came to ask the snake why he attacked the inhabitants of the local village. The serpent fell silent, not knowing the answer why. Only that it was in his nature to strike upon any passerby. The serpent was so moved by his self-realization that he resolved to never again attack anyone in the village.

A month later, the sage returned to the same village. Everyone was happy because they no longer lived in fear of the deadly serpent. Everyone, except the serpent. When the sage went back to the little grove to visit the snake, he found the creature hiding in darkness with bruises and cuts all over his body. The snake blamed the sage for his state, saying that ever since the sage told him to not bite and attack people, everyone in the village threw rocks and sticks and stones whenever they saw him. Because they were no longer afraid of him, the children would come and taunt him. It was because of the sage's wise advice that he was in this state.

The sage calmly replied, "I told you not to bite people. I did not say that you could not hiss".

I live by the hiss, a far safer alternative than the poisonous bite. As a small, brown girl—an immigrant bullied by those bigger and "different" from me, assuming a "hissing"-like position was the greatest defense that I had. I find that it is still useful to ward off unwanted attention and malicious intentions. Over the years I developed my own brand of a "hiss"-like vibe that envelopes me whenever I feel unsafe or uncomfortable. A hiss-like sensation that warns others to back off, creating an invisible bubble of security around myself.

***

A "hiss" is not just onomatopoeic; the word and the acoustic vibration it designates do not only entail a sonic quality. A "hiss" can also be sensational, where the sound has a tactile quality that warms the blood and discomforts the skin at its deepest cellular level. I only first learned about this quality of the hiss in my early twenties through my advanced Bharatanatyam training. The artform is most recognized for its codified and strict movements, forcing unnatural strains on the lower back, knees and hips that I know will cause me problems later in life. But balancing the strictness of form and movement is the freedom of emotive interpretation, where the dancer is expected to pantomime the deepest depths and complexity of emotion for the various protagonists and characters who are the subjects of different songs.

Early in their training, dancers are primarily taught songs that recount stories of various Hindu mythological epics, providing the space for the dancer to embody a god, hero, human, or demon—a sometimes quick transformation that enables the individual to practice the feeling of capturing the full range of actions and emotions within a story. While these roles have an importance unto themselves within the larger cannon of dance dramas and ballets, their emotive scope paled in comparison to the much more subtle nuances that came from portraying an ordinary woman. Not a special woman, like a goddess or a princess, but an ordinary woman navigating love, independence, societal expectations, and her relationships with men and other women. No other role exposes the vulnerabilities of the self. And yet no other role shakes you to your core, providing another language and channel to express the quietest sadness or the loudest rage.

My first encounter with the uneasy familiarity of playing an ordinary woman came during my teenage years, learning songs that sang the plight of a young adolescent girl experiencing the bloom of first love. As the epitome of teenage awkwardness, I struggled with throwing my body into acting and revealing the realization of a romantic crush in front of others. The struggle then was not out of lack of experiencing those emotions at some level within myself. Instead, they came from a general sense of insecurity and lack of confidence that commonly plagues adolescence, especially if you were routinely labeled by all of the adult women in your life as "the late bloomer." I did at some point finally bloom, though it was far less exciting because it happened years after many of my peers reached that stage. Yet the delay gave me more time to process my emotions, and to give my body time to catch up with my head and my heart. In many ways, I had the extra time I needed to prepare myself to take on more challenging pieces that explored the inner emotional lives of these everyday women, who despite living in the past eerily felt like my own contemporaries.

Within the tradition, there are eight kinds of *nāyikā*—female protagonists and heroines who speak and dance out their inner emotions, allowing them to reflect on their romantic relationships while also think about their own lives as women with complex inner selves. Each kind of *nāyikā* is featured across various songs and poems, the bulk of which were composed between the sixteenth and seventeenth centuries, a time when expressions of passion and erotic love were not subject to the scrutiny and criticism that accompanied European colonialism. As my training in dance progressed, I found it easier to connect and understand most of the *nāyikās*, primarily after having experienced similar feelings and situations. I felt the first blooms of love, sometimes too many times than I care to admit. Such moments were inevitably followed by the despair that loomed over a broken relationship. Then there was the feeling of betrayal, or anger at an ex-lover or boyfriend. I could even conceptualize some of the more esoteric *nāyikās*, such as the ever-faithful woman, who patiently awaits her lover's return.

But there was one *nāyikā* that fascinated me, and continues to hold my imagination till this day. *Virahokaṇḍitha nāyikā*—the heroine suffering the pangs of separation, away from her lover. Her essence is defined by *viraham*—a boundless and never-ending longing that seeps into every fiber of her being. *Viraham* is more than just a mental, psychological state. It has the power to distort time, space, and matter for the heroine and everyone in her world. Within dance, there are many ways to convey this separation and longing. Some are literal— the heroine can't eat or sleep. Some reflect a distortion of the world, where things that were once beautiful suddenly become gruesome and grotesque. My favorite way to depict this longing, however, is through poetic analogy. In this depiction, I would show how the evening breezes, meant to be cooling after the long intense heat of the subcontinental sun, no longer produced the same refreshment and respite that it once did. Instead, the breezes were harsh and could burn, a sensation comparable to heat that escapes a viper's hiss. It is a burning sensation that consumes the entire body, mind, and soul, making even the most forgiving of fabrics almost unbearable to wear. But the heat serves as a reminder for the heroine, tormenting her into never forgetting the distance that separates her from her love, and forcing her to confront the various incarnations that longing can take.

***

Covid-19 and the quarantine that followed created the conditions for a now unending separation and longing that I can never seem to fully escape. When the world shut down for the first time, I would wake up, feeling the blood rush into my face as I was drenched in sweat from a nightmare. I was imprisoned within a sick psychological loop, constantly thinking about the state of the world, only to work myself up to not dwell on the impending doom that came with each succeeding day. I would leave my house to get milk, and found myself completely disoriented by the outside world. I was lost and useless, without a will to engage or get enraged.

Emotionally processing the unmoored and detached existence I was living helped me appreciate how painful those pangs of separation might have been for those poets and *nayikās* of the past. I could not eat or sleep. I could not find beauty in things that I once enjoyed. Living each day of the quarantine felt like a burden, not knowing what I was supposed to do with myself or even how I could live in this limbo-like existence.

At the time, I was living in Michigan, maintaining my self-quarantine away from my close friends. But I was also living alone away from my family across the border in Canada. Never again will I take for granted the proximity of that border. While I lived in Michigan, going home to see my family was an easy affair. After a short one-hour drive, I was already in another country, and well on my way to reconnecting with my kin and close family friends. The threshold that separated my professional from personal life was not only invisible, it also felt insignificant. But now, crossing that boundary felt like a multi-day journey of quest-like proportions, as if I had to scale some sort of insurmountable barrier to reconnect with my closest family and friends.

I remember being told by one of my cousin-brothers after about a month of quarantine that in some ways, were very lucky. We were Millennials, living in the new millennium with all of the comforts and advances of communication technology, enabling us to still stay in touch and connect with others in the new contact-free world that had become the new normal. In some ways, he was right. The *nayikās* of the past after all, could not Facetime or Zoom with their lovers. There was no mediated alternative to reach out and create a channel of connection. Instead, they were alone, suffering day after day till they received some sign that indicated their lover's imminent return.

Like others, I took quickly to the Zoom and Skype nights, making the most of the medium to stay in touch with as many people as

I could. Soon, days and evenings became filled with my own kind of digital social calendar, each night occupied with some virtual happy hour, a virtual dinner, or virtual conversation over UberEats followed by a Netflix or Amazon watch party. They helped no doubt, through offering some small relief to the isolation that came from quarantine. But the small swells of happiness that came with each virtual reunion only made it more apparent, and more unbearable, the ultimate lack of connection and connectivity that was in my life. The emotional weight of separation left an uneasy sensation throughout body. Though I tried to ignore it, I could feel the hairs on my neck and arm tingle, lightly burning from a silent hiss that I could hear in the distance.

In these songs and poems, the only cure for the pains of separation is reunification. Being brought together with that person, thing, and feeling that was once estranged from you. In the end, there is no substitution for co-presence. Simulations composed of bits, bytes, and pixels very quickly fall short of the totality of feelings that you can only get from being with others, physically next to each other in the world. It is a chemical magnetism—a sensation that comes from inhabiting the same time and space with the people, things, and places that you miss the most. There is an excitement that comes from being around others. You can feel it in the quickening of your heart, to the lightness of your step. It generates a euphoria that can quiet and calm the restless soul, while serving as the antidote to soothe the burns that came from a serpent's hiss.

***

There are some kinds of reunifications however that are still too painful to wade through. Instead of feeling the respite that was hoped for, more sorrow and emotional hopelessness is revealed. You do not get the respite and catharsis of returning to how things once were. Instead, you are left feeling stupid, naïve, arrogant, or immature to think that there ever could be the happy reunion and fulfilment to your separation and longing. Instead, you realize how that feeling, person, and situation that you dramatized and recreated in your mind for so long was simply a foolish dream to help you forget not only the pain you were feeling in the moment, but also the tragic and traumatic events that you wished to escape.

I remember the moment in the pandemic when this realization hit me the most and hardest. It was December of 2020, and I was able to spend almost a month with my mother, the first time that I was able to see her and pass time with her since the pandemic started. I had hoped for it to be the cathartic release of reunification that I had long dreamt of. I could not have been more wrong. Naturally, when you put two South Asian women in a space together, intensity will automatically burst forth and fill the room with that emotional energy and tension. In that month I saw the ways that my mother's spirit and zest for life had further diminished.

It was an already fading light, one that has taken years of emotional abuse and underappreciation from friends and family. I remember being in my late teens, and beginning to see her go through these depressive episodes, only to see them increase as the years went on. Yet in her own way, she rejected these lows, continuing to push herself to hold things together for my brother, father, and others in our family. That month revealed another new low, where she barely kept herself together for the sake of my visit home. But I could tell that the months of quarantining, of being isolated, and being alienated and separated away from people she once held close had really hit her hard. She started to recall bad memories, experiences of emotional and verbal abuse from her father and her husband that she hid from us, never sharing them but suffering in silence. She was always one of the more progressive members of my family—a feminist even though she never had called herself by that term. But human beings are contradictions, and my mother is perhaps one of the most puzzling ones that ever walked this earth, convincing herself to stay in an emotionally hurtful marriage for the sake of maintaining her values, and upholding the primacy of duty that comes with being a South Asian wife and mother.

Those were months of darkness that accompanies the trying winters of the northeast, where daylight is as scarce a resource as diversity is in Vermont. While I was worried about her, I partially attributed her new lows to the weather, which can make even the most ardent optimist question the meaning of their own existence. "Things will turn around, they will be better in the future!"—I feel foolish even now as I hear this hollow promise for a brighter, more optimistic world to come. But how could I not feel a little ray of hope? Why should I not have allowed myself the pleasure of letting my guard down? There were things that I thought were worth celebrating, in spite of the horrors that continued to rage in the world outside us. I somehow managed to get a stable job that was the start to a new career and new life for myself. I was starting to make a life for myself as an independent adult. Perhaps it was my stupidity, or maybe my selfishness, but I thought it was time to finally celebrate myself, and invite others to do so with me, after so many years of sidelining my own accomplishments for the needs, priorities, and achievements of others in my family.

My mother quickly shattered that narrative, finding the crack of narcissistic folly in the mirror that reflected these visions and swiftly inflicting the precise blow to see it all crumble away. Presenting my mother with these misplaced hopes revived a constant struggle between us. I would present my happiness and excitement for things happening in my life—things that I should be happy and proud about. In response, I receive a stoic "Yes, that is fine." A tearful, emotional argument ensues about why she can't be happy or excited for me. Sadness turns into anger and resentment, asking her why all her responses to my happiness is some version of "Oh … ok. Well good for you." At some point in these arguments, she breaks down—reminding me of the emptiness of her life, the constant hurt she endures, and how emotionally trapped she feels. It is a gaslighting that I constantly put up with out of love for my mother, and the very real acceptance of the ways that she has been worn down over her life. Yet today, I resolve to not concede to my mother, to apologize to her for being selfish and not considering her needs. Mentally, I am prepared to counter these well-worn arguments by saying something along the lines of "But this time it is really different! Why can't you accept that?"

It was different. But not because I felt that for once we should feel happy and hopeful. Instead, the difference came in how my mother broke down. She held back her tears, letting only one escape down her cheek. Slowly and almost inaudibly, she whispered, "Because, I have nothing left in me to give." I know that my mother was trying to project strength. Instead, she looked lower, sadder, and more emotionally fractured. She looked like a broken vase that was hastily glued back together. The outer shape resembled its original form. But you could tell that it was barely being held together by the cheap glue used to connect is dismembered parts, its compositional integrity too compromised to withstand even the slightest touch. At that moment, she was a whole woman who was moments away from crumbling, dispersing fragments of herself across the floor.

***

I remember at the start of the pandemic, finding comfort and solace in one of my mentors and close friends. An immigrant who was raised in France, she had grown up with stories of the hardships and sacrifices that family members had made in order to survive the two world wars that ravaged her country. As a way to put things in perspective, she slowly and cautiously pointed out to me that this pandemic was our generation's war.

I am sure that at one time in history, or perhaps in our mythic history, there was something truly called a just war, or a war fought on noble grounds. I grew up with mythological stories about wars, that were fought between good and evil, where the victor is able to restore order, duty, and morality back in the world. But the wars of man are not fought on nearly as noble grounds, if one can call any such conflict truly noble. Even more, wars are not generous or restorative. Instead, they are selfish, demanding more from their people than what they give back to them in return. They require sacrifice, loss, death, and destruction, for the benefit of a few over the lives of so many others.

Wars always begin with the hubris that once the conflict is over and the dust settles, order will be restored and life will go back to "normal." That is after all, the human narrative we wish for. Good and righteous triumphs over bad, and we all can then go back to living happily ever after. History, or at least a pragmatic, realistic outlook shows the ways that we can never really "go back" to the ways things were before the conflict, struggle, and sacrifice. Some of the changes that emerge from wars lead to societal changes that modernist versions of history frame as a lesson in social and cultural progress, where we become more open, tolerant, or just a better version of ourselves. But these narratives occlude the many stories of isolation, alienation, depression, and instability that comes from a world trying to go back to some version of itself that is now long buried along with the other dead casualties of war.

***

Days pass, and the extreme quarantine measures soon begin to lift. Travel is possible, albeit difficult, and runs its own kinds of risks.

Physical co-presence is permitted, but under strict and limiting circumstances. I am able to see people in person, and even laugh at times. I move house a couple times during this period, and am lucky to meet and develop new, deep friendships with people who welcome me in their homes and lives. A veneer of normalcy begins to settle. But it is a light coat, like the first flurries of winter that leave a dusting on the sidewalks and streets, only to be blown away by the lightest breeze, erasing their existence from view.

We are told that life needs to go on, and so we try. We get vaccinated, travel, and see people. I make another larger move across the country. I meet new friends, go out, and even gather in "crowds" that at one point were thought to be the kiss of death. I am moving on, but I don't know from what or even where. For me, the rhythms of each day seem to be a continuation of the circadian rhythms that I had unwillingly grown accustomed to from the early days of quarantining. Superficially, I feel like everything has returned to being the same as before. Yet deep in my heart I feel a tugging of how much has changed, and how nothing is right. Nothing is like the way it was before. The malaise that engulfed my life seems to continue extending its presence into this new phase and chapter of my life. Like an elasticized shroud, I continue to feel it hanging over my body. To no avail, it finds new ways of stretching. And I know that I will be the one to break first.

I see it in the little things. I hear it in the exhaustion in my voice when I call people on the phone. Sometimes I forgo the desire to connect entirely, too tired to want to talk to people in general. My interest, or even passing enjoyment, in shows that I once carelessly binged no longer brings the same satisfaction. Outfits that once empowered me; sartorial ensembles carefully constructed to walk that fine line between powerful, fun, and flirty, have lost all visual appeal when I look at myself in the mirror. Even going out and being around others, a ritual that I once relished and looked forward to, now has the opposite effect of making me feel more alone. Seeking the company of friends and family feels often like a tiring chore than some recuperative measure to make me feel whole again, and to help me feel like the person I once was.

Loss of appetite. Avoiding the company of others. Fading interest in finding beauty in things that previously captured the aesthetic pleasure centers of my mind. The longing and pain of separation for my inner *nāyikā* seems to have not abated. I have been able to see my friends, family, and even return to doing some of the things that I loved the most. Yet what is this longing, this *viraham*, that continues to unsettle my daily routine and attempts of emotional equanimity?

***

Life is still moving on. I am in this new phase; new job, new place in life. I have made new friendships. And I met someone who cares about me, who helps me find something to laugh about at the end of each day, no matter how hard or terrible each one might be. He too has his own stories of sadness and despair that have also transformed into another kind of melancholy and trauma that was brought on by Covid and the endless pandemic. We find a comfort in being there for each other. And yet, I find that I approach these good fortunes with an air of realism, no longer filled with aspirational nostalgia of the past. I treat my job as simply another opportunity to grow as a scholar and writer. And I approach my relationship from the perspective of understanding the person I am with. Not hoping that he will live up to the romantic visions of what I once thought and hoped I might have. Instead, I strive to see him and love him for who he is, rough edges and all. And despite all of that, he continues to be there for me, showing a goodness and constancy that I find more endearing than any of the passionate volatility that existed in boyfriends and relationships of the past. It is not the whirlwind romantic story that my pre-pandemic self would have hoped for. Instead, it is a relationship grounded in small simple gestures, each one that says that he cares despite the uncertainty and lack of control that he also feels in his life.

I suppose that is the affectual state of our generation, and it will always be infused into both our lives for many years to come. And yet, there is a realness to our happiness together, perhaps because it comes from a place of brutal, honest realism of who we are and the world we live in today, instead of ideals that came from our younger selves. In some ways, I have become my own kind of *nāyikā*, my own kind of heroine who is not only constantly trying to understand the complexities of life and love in our current world, but also experimenting with new ways to express those discoveries, sharing it with others in the hopes that I do not feel the burden of navigating these challenges all alone.

As I write this, I am still quite young. Yet I can't help but look back at the youthful optimism that I once had before the world had even heard of Covid-19. There was a willful innocence and ignorance that I felt that I had to have since I still had so much life to live. Now, I find I am slowly giving up my longing from that version of myself, as a means of survival to avoid feeling distraught. These are all emotional preventative measures that I have developed, helping me cope when those feelings of longing for my prior world intensify, and with the emotional fallout when those feelings and visions do not live up to the demands and needs of the world that I live in now. Like the advice the sage gave to snake, I do not need to live the most extreme vision or version of myself in order to fulfill my true nature. Just as the snake realized the unnecessity of attacking others to assert its dominance, so too am I learning to adjust my own expectations, moving away from the dreams and hopes I had as a young girl and shifting towards a newer set of goals and perhaps even a different journey on the path that lies ahead. Slowly, those pains and feelings of listlessness are subsiding.

And yet, every now and then, I still feel a warming sensation brush against my skin, slightly unsettling my soul. It knows how to pull deep into my heartstrings, seeking out some remnant of the false visions of the world that I once thought I needed like an emotional crutch, in order to survive on my own terms in this world. It tantalizes my basic instincts and tendencies, tempting me to reconcile with my old self and encouraging me to take refuge in the old yearnings that once provided a false sense of comfort. But when this happens, I just take a deep breath, slowly releasing the air out of my lungs. Listen carefully, and you can hear how my controlled exhale bears a slight resemblance to a hiss.

Roxana Cazan

Mothers, Mother-Work, and the Pandemic: A Quick Look at Gender Inequality in the Twenty-First Century

Screened as part of *Brooklyn, USA*, "Pandemic Motherhood" is a 2020 short documentary film in which writer, director, and producer Shaina Feinberg interviews nine Brooklyn-based working mothers about their experiences with motherhood during the pandemic. The nine interviewed mothers speak about the ways in which the lockdown and closure of schools have profoundly changed their lives, from daily schedules to self-image, from attitude about life to relationships with others. The mothers speak about being emotionally distanced from their children, lacking a structure to their days, lacking privacy and time alone, being angry with those around them, feeling defeated and discouraged. The nine women suggest that the many tasks that the pandemic suddenly assigned them, from raising and educating children to managing the household, confine them to roles that prohibit other types of agency similar to those of their partners. Describing her spouse's work schedule, one woman explains that her wife's job demands render her completely unavailable to participate in mother-work. Another interviewee argues that not only during the pandemic but also prior to this global crisis, society and governments have done nothing to support motherhood, that is to help mothers exist as independent humans with access to an identity and agency outside their mothering roles.

Clearly, these women are not alone, despite their location (Brooklyn represents a unique environment for the social construction of gender and gender roles). Contrary to these women, I am a Romanian immigrant who lives in Oklahoma, a space where expectations regarding gender roles are highly influenced by traditional religious values, conservative political attachments, and a rural physical landscape. However, all the mothers I interact with express very similar concerns. The film director presents these confessions as a form of therapy. While the comfort of knowing one is not alone constitutes a powerful coping mechanism, it does not alter the fact that mother-work, particularly during the pandemic, continues to be expected of women and contributes to reinforcing the inequity between genders in the private sphere.

Many articles have already highlighted the ways in which the pandemic has reignited dialogue over gender inequality. The BBC, the NPR, and other major news agencies have suggested that the pandemic has regressed feminist work by decades. For instance, Pallavi Gogoi[2] writing for NPR argues that the pandemic revealed a form of systemic inequality in the private sphere, where working women, exhausted by the demands of childcare and housework, have been forced to quit their jobs four times more than men in 2020. In a research study for the McKinsey Institute, Anu Madgavkar, Olivia White, Mekala Krishnan, Deepa Mahajan, and Xavier Azcue[3] suggest that the burden of unpaid care is already disproportionately carried by women, and the pandemic only exacerbated this burden, especially for those women who lost their jobs. They write, "in a gender-regressive scenario in which no action is taken to counter these effects, we estimate that global [gross domestic product] growth could be $1 trillion lower in 2030 than it would be if women's unemployment simply tracked that of men in each sector."

Amanda Taub[4] writes for the *New York Times* that "Substantial research has shown that most professional gender gaps are in fact motherhood gaps: women without children are much closer to parity with men when it comes to salaries and promotions, but mothers pay a large career penalty." Taub explains that poor, minority, or immigrant mothers have been affected by pandemic lockdowns more severely than white, middle-class mothers. "Poorer families tend to have more parity between the parents' earnings. But they rely on both incomes to survive and are also more likely to have jobs that must be done in-person rather than remotely. When schools and daycares close, there is no one to care for young children or supervise older ones' remote schooling if both parents work. But if one stays home, the family faces financial catastrophe." Center for American Progress contributors, Julie Kashen, Sarah Jane Glynn, and Amanda Novello[5] underscore that despite lockdown requirements that eliminated child care options for millions of parents, "As a result of a variety of factors, including policy choices grounded in racism and sexism, low-wage workers, solo mothers, and women of color—three groups with considerable overlap—are all too often not in the economic position to leave the paid labor force to care for their children." They suggest that, in general, the decrease in maternal labor force participation caused by the pandemic would undo the past twenty-five years of feminist progress.

My own personal experience corroborates these arguments. I became a mother only a few months before the pandemic had officially reached Europe and North America. Because my husband is gainfully employed in Oklahoma, and to ensure our son's smooth introduction to the world (he had battled a life-threatening infection at birth), we had determined that I would stay home and care for our son until the baby turns one. As first-generation immigrants, I had no extended family support, and the inequitable and gendered division of labor had already constructed me as a less-valuable work agent in the public sphere. My field of expertise has also recently been devalued, despite my numerous terminal degrees, including a PhD in English, a phenomenon visibly attested by the permanent or temporary dissolutions of academic humanities departments[6] and the recent layoffs[7] of tenured university professors across the USA. Unable to make as much money as my husband and proficient in an area that doesn't directly service the capitalist machine of wealth accumulation, I became the logical choice of childcare provider in my family. The gender inequality became apparent to me particularly as my husband's demanding job requires most of his waking hours, leaving me in charge not only of childcare but also homecare and household management, additional responsibilities for which I do not have a predilection based solely on my gender or ability to reproduce. However, all of these adjacent tasks inflect and determine my mother-work.

When I first met my husband, I was stunned by his commitment to gender equity and equality, first as the lead of an academic program that has traditionally excluded women (petroleum and natural gas engineering), and second as a heterosexual man in the intimate setting. However, despite his commitment to hiring women and supporting female and women-identified students as he built a new academic program at a small university in Pennsylvania, his attitude about equal housework, or his enthusiastic support of all my creative and scholarly pursuits, something changed in 2020. I was a new mother, overwhelmed by the frequency of nursing, controlled by a compulsion to sanitize our home, and simply and abundantly exhausted. Our child had spent about a week in the newborn intensive care unit (NICU) at Saint Anthony's Hospital in Oklahoma City where he had contracted a terrible infection only a few hours after delivery. Anxious to ensure this episode would never recur despite Covid-19, I took charge of childcare and housework because I was convinced that only if I cleaned the floor myself could I be certain that my son's bouncer seat would not be instantly colonized by microbes; only if I scrubbed and sterilized each bottle every time it was used would I be able to ensure that the milk my son drank would not cause him any harm; only if I laundered his clothes, sheets, and blankets at the beginning and end of each day could I be certain my son will stay healthy. The trauma of the NICU ushered in a new anxiety for me, one that I claimed as mine alone, not being able to allow my spouse the space to come to terms with his own trauma as a co-parent. However, this behavior reinforced my role as primary caretaker of child and home, thus connecting me to a gender role both my husband and I had resisted. Inevitably, my profound discontent with my newly acquired role directed my anger towards my husband, who became not only complicit with the *status quo* but also the ruling patriarch in a system meant to keep me entrenched!

Pandemic and birth story aside, motherhood is a contested domain marked by multiple investments, commitments, or disavowals that can produce myriad forms of maternal agency. Motherhood yields mother-work, a concept developed by feminist scholars such as Andrea O'Reilley, Sharon Hays, or Sara Ruddick. Ruddick argues that "mothers are not identified by the fixed biological or legal relationship to their children but by the work they set out to do."[8] This kind of "caring labor" underlies the assumptions that mothers are inherently loving. Mother-work does not require a particular sexual commitment, household arrangement, or birthing ability. However, despite the value placed on a woman who chooses to stay at home with children, particularly in the South (Oklahoma included), the real value of a mother's work is transparent in the construction of childcare as unremunerative employment. And if before the pandemic, mother-work had been rendered invisible because the private sphere remained inaccessible to the public eye, with the increasing use of technologies that penetrate the private (such as Zoom meetings, for instance), the value and nature of mother-work have become more visible. While the pandemic enhanced the burden of mother-work, it did not necessarily undo decades worth of accomplished equality between genders because equality, arguably, never truly existed.

Why mother-work? For many decades, feminist scholars have concentrated exclusively on the production of commodities even as they admitted that reproductive life and reproductive work or mother-work rest at the core of any transformative project. Mother-work is central not only to capitalist accumulation but also to any form of organization. Feminists in the 1970s spoke of mother-work in terms of domestic work, to refer to all activities that reproduce our daily lives and labor-power. Procreation is part of reproduction, but so is the reproduction of the workforce, which takes place both inside and outside the home (in schools, hospitals, etc.). More recently, feminists have also determined that in communities that rely more heavily on agriculture, mother-work and reproduction begin with putting seeds in the soil and caring for the environment, and this is why discussions about ecological degradation necessarily involve women. To take it a step further, since women compose the network of primary care, whether this be at home or at the hospital, a pandemic requires that we consider its implications on reproduction and mother-work.

That the pandemic aggravated the gender division of labor (with or without the lockdown) becomes apparent when considering essential and frontline workers whose reproduction of care work entails the "packing and delivering [of] supplies, caring for the sick and elderly, and keeping streets and buildings clean." An Associated Press census data analysis[9] indicates that this burden has been borne unevenly across gender, racial, and socioeconomic lines, with women of color and immigrant women most likely to "mak[e] social life and culture [within the pandemic] possible" as Luce Irigaray would suggest.[10] Given that official discourse about the pandemic has been produced and controlled by men—from Dr. Fauci, Robert Ray Redfield (former Director of the Centers for Disease Control and Prevention), or William Brockmann Long (former administrator of the Federal Emergency Management Agency) to the President—it appears that the market order dictated by the pandemic maintains, by and large, similar patriarchal mechanisms of exchange as the social order to which second-wave feminists, such as Luce Irigaray just mentioned, responded. Although the pandemic shifted the ways in which market exchanges take place, women continue to remain unremunerated laborers in the private sphere where they tend to be responsible for care and mother-work. Despite a substantial increase in childcare done by men during the pandemic, women are still doing the majority of the additional home childcare.[11]

The preference for patriarchal gender roles during the pandemic has also been noted by Daniel L. Rosenfeld and A. Janet Tomiyama at the University of California, Los Angeles. They argue that "During the pandemic, participants reported conforming more strongly to traditional gender roles and believing more strongly in traditional gender stereotypes than they did before the pandemic. Political ideology remained constant over time. These findings suggest that a pandemic may promote preference for traditional gender roles."[12] The authors refer to system justification theory—a theory within social psychology that defends the social *status quo*—arguing that "environmental uncertainty can promote conservatism by motivating a need for structure, … a resistance to social change," and a desire to "defend social systems in the face of … instability and change." Scholars have also invoked evolutionary reasoning to explain the large-scale backslide towards traditional gender norms during the pandemic. In an editorial written for *Frontiers in Sociology*, entitled "Patriarchy and Populism during the COVID-19 Pandemic," Carol C. Gould of Hunter College, City University of New York, writes about the patriarchal politics of the pandemic being enhanced by patriarchal and authoritarian forms of populism.[13]

Analyzing one form of populism that escalated over the past year, Lorna Bracewell[14] of Flagler College argues that QAnon supporters, for instance, tend to identify with one of two traditional gender categories either as "masculine protectors of the republic who swear an oath to defend the Constitution and become 'digital soldiers' in Q's army" or "as feminine guardians of hearth and home who organize rallies and social media campaigns to protect children from sexual and moral contamination." The problem is that populist movements produce women as auxiliaries to men. Motherhood and reproduction in this context have then two contradictory outcomes: they produce [women] as people on the one hand and as exploitable sidekicks on the other hand.[15]

The pandemic, however, has struck not only mothers' access to agency over their own bodies, but also their ability to navigate matrescence and embrace the new persons they have become *postpartum*. Lucia

Rocca-Ihenacho and Cristina Alonso study the pandemic repercussions on safety during childbirth, and argue that "Women's rights in childbirth are being threatened by lack of care during labor, restrictions on accompaniment, unnecessary interventions including inductions, separation of mother and baby and prohibition on breastfeeding."[16] In an article published in *Nature*, Clare Watson underscores that because the pandemic limited women's access to antenatal care, the numbers of stillbirths have increased over the past year.[17] Considering the number of births per capita, the *Financial Times* announces a sharp decline in births during the pandemic. However, when mothers do give birth during the pandemic, their experience of *postpartum* is characterized by physical separation and emotional trauma enhanced by the hormonal output after birth.

An opinion piece in the *Atlantic* by Sophie Gilbert argues that the isolation a mother experiences when giving birth during the pandemic constitutes one outcome of a larger phenomenon according to which viruses "punish intimacy."[18] The article cites a line from a novel written by Lawrence Wright that Ebola specifically targets love and compassion. Like Ebola, then, the coronavirus has separated families, left people to die all alone, and forced mothers to give birth by themselves. In the subtitle, Gilbert confesses another consequence of becoming a mother during the pandemic: "This completely different person I've become since I gave birth is someone virtually no one knows." Not only are *postpartum* women affected by the hormonal avalanche that overtakes the brain, but also the community typically formed by the birth attendants (partners, family member, friends) and meant to serve as a social buffer of the kind "we are in this together; you are not alone," is missing. The mother birthing alone emerges as a transformed human, both literally considering the physical changes in the body, and metaphorically, in existential terms. But no one has witnessed this intimate transformation, so something of the bond with loved ones that motherhood can create is wasted.

Numerous birthing advice articles issued during the pandemic list women's rights while giving birth as a response to the pandemic restrictions in hospitals: the right to choose their medical provider, the right to have a partner or support person present, the right to stay with the newborn, the right to breastfeed. Articulated as rights, these healthcare practices reveal that the pandemic not only punishes intimacy and compassion, but also affects the ways in which people understand citizenship. That "re-open" protests have occurred with regularity across in the US in 2020 is amply documented. The rhetoric of these protest movements, however, evinces the tenets of right-wing populism that frame the opposition people versus government elites, work versus welfare, and independence versus dependence. Populism has already set up the space for demonizing public health practices, so that when the pandemic required hospitals to rethink public access, these transformations could be easily understood as limiting access in general as a prohibition to constitutional rights. Social media platforms hosted a high number of debates over mask wearing and social distancing, especially when these public health measures would affect the ways in which one typically enacts their celebratory citizenship as during July 4th festivities. Therefore, when women are told that federal or state entities prevent their access to practices typically taken for granted, it is not impossible to imagine that some may feel threatened in their access to their rights.

Perhaps the most invisible aftermath of the pandemic is its consequence on women's and mothers' access to citizenship and their relationship with the state. Because citizenship grants one access to legal protection and equality through active engagement in political or social life, "violence against women is recognized as an issue for the state, citizenship, and the whole community."[19] Scholars noted an increase in domestic sexual violence during the pandemic. For example, Caroline Bradbury-Jones writes about home as a space where dynamics of power can be subverted by abusers without scrutiny from the outside or from the larger family.[20] Religious, conservative, and nationalist discourse lends the concept of family "sanctity," thus speaking about abuse within the domestic sphere, especially between intimate partners, comes with great difficulty for many victims. The stringent lockdown restrictions then restrict individuals' avenues of escape from abuse and allow children to witness abuse more directly. Sediri *et al.* argue that because women tend to be the victims of domestic abuse more so than men (although men can suffer abuse as can partners in same-sex or gender-complex relationships), women have reported most mental distress during the pandemic, all the while unable to seek help.[21]

Imagine Ramona, a mother of two young children, the recipient of periodic bouts of physical violence from her partner. Imagine that Ramona lives in a small home and has no access to child care. Perhaps she is also unemployed. Day in and out, she homeschools her children, handles all housework, and constantly calls or emails different local government offices to find out how she could get more help with rent payments. She is very worried and exhausted. The trauma of the pandemic adds to the burden of physical violence, and one night after a beating, Ramona does not know what to do. She fears for her life, and she just wants a break. So, she grabs her car keys and drives away, knowing that her partner is usually gentle with the children. But the neighbors who have already called the police over to Ramona's apartment, call again to report that Ramona ran away and left the children with the monster. The following morning, when the partner leaves for work, Ramona returns. She is more tired than ever, needs a shower and a cup of hot coffee. She kisses her children who are just waking up when the doorbell rings. It's the child protection people and the police, both alerted by the nosy albeit well-intended neighbor. How can Ramona mother in this situation?

As my colleague at the University of Oklahoma, Dr. Meg Sibbett, argues,[22] state determinations of "failure to protect" charges against mothers surviving domestic abuse project the state (and the nosy neighbor) as a benevolent protector of children and simultaneously an agent of intimate terrorism for women like Ramona, struggling to survive abuse and maintain custody of their children. When an abused woman is charged with neglect for another person's actions, she becomes alienated from a "system" that is supposed to protect her. Studies also indicate that Failure to Protect Laws are disproportionately enforced against women, and most of these women are mothers.[23] The state's project of protecting children from "bad" mothers normalizes the benevolent violence of the state against women in abusive situations, which as data indicates, has increased exponentially during the pandemic.

Let me then return to the short documentary with which I opened. The frame Feinberg employs to situate her interviews depicts an eight-year-old boy energetically dancing and running through the house. The voice narrating over interprets the scenes as exhausting and despair-inducing. The same voice qualifies the interviews as therapeutic for the simple fact that they echo the narrator's despondency. However, before we are offered this frame at the beginning of the documentary, the visual cues compare this state of misery to drowning in a terrible flood or to being haunted by a demonic creature. Perhaps in the context of the information presented in the interviews, these scenes may appear hyperbolic. However, they highlight the insidious ways in which the pandemic has encumbered people's bodily and mental integrity, without which one cannot function fully in the public and the private spheres alike. And yet, neither the frame, nor the symbolic scenes preceding it incorporate the actual pandemic. I interpret the absence of the pandemic proper in the images surrounding the interviews as a way through which we can understand that with or without lockdown restrictions, relegating women to roles that encumber their existence as full citizens constitutes a common phenomenon. It is not the pandemic with its "staying at home" exhortation that pushed women back in their journey of equality with men, but rather, this equality has not been reached at a systemic level.

I was fortunate to have the possibility to return to work when my son turned one. I was aided by access to childcare: we were able to hire a nanny and later, having contracted and survived Covid-19 as a family, I and my husband determined that daycare can be an option for our son. (In Oklahoma, Governor Kevin Stitt had urged childcare facilities to stay open, despite the national lockdown.) Returning to work, although dangerous given potential exposure, restored some of my mental health and appeased my *postpartum* anxiety. It also allowed me to feel on a somewhat equal footing with my husband by enabling me to eschew constant participation in mother-work, and by encouraging my husband to participate in care work more so than before. I picked up writing, even though I certainly do not have more time than I did when I stayed at home. I started to feel more autonomous, and honestly, I started to feel more connected to my child, my marriage, and my mother-work.

At the time of research, there was very little data available to describe transgender experiences. However, the research includes references to lesbian couples. More work needs to be done to unpack the experiences of trans parents in the context of parenting roles during the pandemic.

References

1. "Pandemic Motherhood," directed by Shaina Feinberg, 2020 (available at https://vimeo.com/445682975/ accessed March 28, 2023).
2. Gogoi, P., "Stuck-At-Home Moms: The Pandemic's Devastating Toll On Women," October 28, 2020 (available at www.npr.

org/2020/10/28/928253674/stuck-at-home-moms-the-pandemics-devastating-toll-on-women/ accessed March 28, 2023).

3. Madgavkar, A., White, O., Krishnan, M., Mahajan, D. and Azcue, X., "COVID-19 and gender equality: Countering the regressive effects" (available at www.mckinsey.com/featured-insights/future-of-work/covid-19-and-gender-equality-countering-the-regressive-effects/ accessed March 28, 2023).

4. Taub, A., New York Times, "Pandemic Will 'Take Our Women 10 Years Back' in the Workplace," September 26, 2020 (available at: www.nytimes.com/2020/09/26/world/covid-women-childcare-equality.html/ accessed March 28, 2023).

5. Kashen, J., Glynn, S J and Novello, A. "How COVID 19 Sent Women's Workforce Progress Backward," October 30, 2020 (available at www.americanprogress.org/article/covid-19-sent-womens-workforce-progress-backward/ accessed March 28, 2023).

6. Dutt-Ballerstad, R., "Academic Prioritization or Killing the Liberal Arts?" *Inside Higher Ed*, March 1, 2019 (available at www.insidehighered.com/advice/2019/03/01/shrinking-liberal-arts-programs-raise-alarm-bells-among-faculty/ accessed March 28, 2023).

7. Ellis, L., "'A Tremendous Amount of Fear': Will Major Cuts Threaten Research Universities' Work?" *The Chronicle of Higher Education*, December 9, 2020 (available at www.chronicle.com/article/a-tremendous-amount-of-fear-will-major-cuts-threaten-research-universities-work/ accessed March 28, 2023).

8. Ruddick, S., *Maternal Thinking: Toward a Politics of Peace*, Beacon Press, Boston, Mass., 1989.

9. CBS News Moneywatch, "Pandemic's front-line work falls on women, minorities," May 1, 2020 (available at www.cbsnews.com/news/fontline-work-women-minorities-pandemic/ accessed March 28, 2023).

10. Irigaray, L., "Women on the Market," *French Feminism Reader*, edited by Kelly Oliver. Rowman & Littlefield, New York, 2000, p. 212.

11. Sevilla, A. and Smith, S., "Baby Steps: the Gender Division of Childcare during the COVID-19 Pandemic." *Oxford Review of Economic Policy*, August 29, 2020, doi: 10.1093/oxrep/graa027.

12. Rosenfeld, D. and Tomiyama, A.J., "Can a Pandemic Make People More Socially Conservative? Political Ideology, Gender Roles, and the Case of COVID-19." *Journal of Applied Social Psychology*, 2021, doi: 10.1111/jasp.12745

13. Gould, C.C., "Editorial: Patriarchy and Populism During the COVID-19 Pandemic," *Frontiers in Sociology*, vol. 6, 2021 (available at www.frontiersin.org/articles/10.3389/fsoc.2021.722393, accessed March 28, 2023).

14. Bracewell, L., "Gender, Populism, and the QAnon Conspiracy Movement," *Frontiers in. Sociology* 5: 615727, 2021, doi.org/10.3389/fsoc.2020.615727.

15. Sitrin, M., "Social Reproduction: Between the Wage and the Commons."

Interview. *Roar Magazine,* 2016 (available at https://truthout.org/articles/social-reproduction-between-the-wage-and-the-commons/ accessed March 28, 2023).

16. Rocca-Ihenacho, L. and Alonso, C., "Where do women birth during a pandemic? Changing perspectives on Safe Motherhood during the COVID-19 pandemic," *Journal of Global Health Science,* 2020, doi.org/10.35500/jghs.2020.2.e4.

17. Watson, C., "Stillbirth Rate Rises Dramatically during Pandemic," *Nature,* 2020 (available at www.nature.com/articles/d41586-020-02618-5/ accessed March 28, 2023).

18. Gilbert, S., "Becoming a Parent during the Pandemic," *The Atlantic,* 2021 (available at www.theatlantic.com/culture/archive/2021/03/isolation-becoming-new-parent-during-pandemic/618244/ accessed March 28, 2023).

19. Franzway, S., "The Sexual Politics of Citizenship and Violence," *Women's Studies International Forum,* vol. 58, 2016, doi.org/10.1016/j.wsif.2016.04.006.

20. Bradbury-Jones, C., "The Pandemic Paradox: The Consequences of COVID-19 on Domestic Violence," *Journal of Clinical Nursing,* vol. 29, 2020, doi/10.1111/jocn.15296.

21. Sediri, S., Zgueb, Y., Ouanes, S. *et al.,* "Women's Mental Health: Acute Impact of COVID-19 Pandemic on Domestic Violence," *Archives of Women's Mental Health,* vol. 23, 2020. doi.org/10.1007/s00737-020-01082-4.

22. Sibbett, M., "Failure to Protect: How Queer Politics Intervenes in the Logic of Children as Hubs of Security," Gender and Justice Speaker Series, November 3, 2022, University of Oklahoma. Lecture.

23. Mahoney, A., "How Failure to Protect Laws Punish the Vulnerable," *Health Matrix,* vol. 21, no. 1, 2019, p. 441.

Domnica Radulescu

Merciless *"Dor"* and My Three Houses of the Apocalypse

Prologue

When the pandemic struck in the spring of 2020, my understanding of home, of a space of belonging and of my relationship to the countries I was indelibly tied to, shifted dramatically. Like many others I thought often of the meaning and reality of an "apocalypse," an end to everything. Strangely, I did not experience despair or fear, but rather a sense of relief. Suddenly the world quieted, and that silence was both ominous and soothing. I had visions of clearer skies, cleaner oceans, unpolluted horizons. I loved listening to "the sound of silence." News of the suddenly clear water in the canals of Venice with frolicking dolphins made me ecstatic. While American friends were anxiously deploring shortages in the grocery stores, I smiled smugly relying on my two decades of previous experience under a communist dictatorship where gaping, empty, grocery stores and shortages of every possible item from any kind of produce from bread to cheese to toilet paper were not the exception but the norm of our daily lives. And when theater friends cried over the cancellation of their shows due to the pandemic, I felt no regret or resentment whatsoever, even though a much-anticipated immigrant theater festival I was preparing in New York was canceled the very day before the premiere. My theater collaborators and I had just completed a magical rehearsal of the show when the performing arts director announced that all of New York was closing, and no shows were going to be performed anywhere. When people were suddenly dying of this new "plague" at a terrifying rate daily, what did a show or a thousand shows matter? I realized that although the word "apocalypse" came up often in discussions, I had never actually checked the etymology of the word. I love etymologies, diving into the origins of words, grabbing their roots across expanses of history and geographies. For an exiled writer, words can be a comforting home, one that gives back as much as you put into it, a reliable dwelling of the mind. So, when I discovered that the Greek origins of the word apocalypse, "*apokaluptein*," means to "uncover" or to "reveal" a sense of calm washed over me. When I left New York of that ominous March 14th, the city I had been feverishly driving to for various theater projects, from my small Virginia town in the Shenandoah Valley where I had built my career and home, had turned from one of the most alive cities in the world, to a ghost town overnight. It made sense that within the shell of that heavy word that we had come to use as the end of the world, were also the seeds of a new beginning, of something to be uncovered and revealed that had remained covered until that moment. Like everybody else, I was focused on survival and safety for my family and myself. But as an immigrant I also pondered maybe more than I had ever before, on the meanings of home and belonging and what that meant for those of us who had chosen the paths of exile from our birth countries.

Much like Irina in Chekhov's *Three Sisters*, for the quarter of a century I had lived in the small Virginia town where I moved from Chicago for the university job, I have relentlessly dreamed of returning to the vibrancy and roar of the big city, Chicago, New York, Paris. … All right, Moscow not so much, as an east European who grew up under the ominous shadow of the Soviet Union. In the end it took a planetary disaster to make me fully embrace my surroundings, and appreciate their beauty and plenitude, in that baleful spring when the redbuds, dogwoods, lilac trees, and hyacinth flowers were showing off their dazzling colors and scents, indifferent to our human miseries. As I watched my son, who a month earlier had returned from New York jobless with lost film projects, assiduously plant a prolific garden in our backyard, or as I walked in that same yard ridiculously mimicking swim moves in a desperate yearning for my lifelong love affair with water athletics, or better yet, as I worked on a new writing project titled "Love Letters from the Dead," because those catastrophic times opened up all the scarred wounds of my youth in a dictatorship and of my early immigrant years, I wanted to say to Irina or really to my own self: "Stay put sister, the countryside is exactly where you should be right now. You can always Zoom with the city people."

As I walked the empty streets of the small town situated in a crook of the Appalachian Mountains, an equally ferocious sense of combined doom and joy washed over me, combination which wildly confused and decentered me, while also facilitating a new window into the meanings of home, belonging, our relationship to the earth and each other, in a word, a "revelation." The following hybridic pieces of dramatic prose emerged precisely from these revelations and visions.

The Three Houses of the Apocalypse

In a persistent fantasy of mine, I have a house in each of the three countries I am forever tied to. The one I was born and grew up in, cradled in a curl of the Carpathian Mountains, washed by the waters of the Black Sea, irrevocably and deliciously chaotic, incorrigibly sentimental, and tormented by messy histories and ferocious ambitions to be like some other "better" countries in the West. I come from the country of this special word pronounced like a breathless exhalation, like a candied scream: "*dor*." I shall call this country number one. Then there is the colossal country made of many countries, where I settled as a political refugee three and a half decades ago and where I made my life, the country whose self-assurance rises to the high heavens and where millions still want to come and live despite the rise of fascism, the barbed wire at its borders, the shameless chasm between the rich and the poor. This would be country number two. And then there is the country of my childhood favorite books, of creamy language, fluffy pastries, lyrical love songs, the country whose culture and literature I have insatiably devoured my entire life, you know, the country of the Eiffel Tower and the juicy kiss that carries its name. And for the sake of correct mathematics this will be referred to as country number three.

House Number One

I ended up in the formidable country number two arriving one frigid December day in the 1980s, as a political refugee from the dictatorship of country number one where I was born and grew up, the one with the candied word of yearning and hopeless melancholy, pronounced like a rushed exhalation like this: "*DOR*."

Something beckoned me to this house like an ancestral echo from unknown ancestors, though nobody in my known history had ever lived in this colossal country before. A life from before, another me that had lived on this wild continent of the buffalo, amidst those old Appalachians, a bison herder, an Amero-Indian princess, a pilgrim from the time of Queen Elizabeth. Maybe I had been there before, and now I was finally coming home to this old house with creaky pine floors, eight fireplaces, bay windows, a wide field in the back marked by a tall oak tree like an old sage, unmoved even in the wildest winds. One day in the twentieth year of my ownership, an apocalypse spread over the entire world and still I loved my house in the country that I don't love so much, even more than before, like a friend, like a magic unshakable shelter which I had to hold on to at any price. I loved the house even more now, as if it protected me from the very country on whose earth it was standing, as if it was floating in a non-country, in a nobody's country space. In my own space, in the amniotic fluids of my imagination. The other me who lived there before, the buffalo herder or the Amero-Indian princess that my spirit inhabited once, told me to hold on to it, she said: *cuddle the hibiscus flowers, caress the maples and the magnolias, tread the earth with care, keep your house warm, but not too warm, your windows clear but with curtains, feed the cardinals, the robins, the woodpeckers, keep putting seeds in the birdfeeders, let the grass and the dandelions grow wild and tall.*

The voices of this future memory in the making started fading and mingling with each other and turning into ethereal characters with feathers, tree branches and bird songs. I could no longer make out which character was saying what, they turned to notes and binaural beats, the words were raindrops and wind gusts, but still they made sense to me. The fact I could make out some meaning from these future whisperings confirmed again that I had to hold on to the special house floating in the universe, whether it was situated on the buffalo territory or in Asia Minor or in the starry heavens. They spoke of our lives and recreated us with better contours than we even had in our lifetimes. It was a *bona fide* collaborative celestial theater project.

What do you remember?

Line up your memories!

The children first.

The woman first too. She owned the house.

The men? How about the men?

They came and went.

They stayed for a while and left singing and zipping up their pants.

She was always there.

How about the other women?

They came and went too buttoning up their blouses?

What was that, some orgy house?

Don't worry about it.

Don't judge anything about them, only the memories matter.

Only the recreation of them matters. The woman and the children.

Let's make a memory competition.

Who wins?

Who comes up with the biggest memory!

Big how, like taking a lot of time or space, what?

A tri-dimensional memory with a beginning, middle and end.

A well-baked memory so we can bring them back in full flesh blood, dress, and boots.

There was once a time when the mother came out in the garden and cried for a long time. The children came after her outside. Then the man living with them at the time came out too and they had an argument. During the time of the argument the children chased each other in the yard. One fell from a tree and hurt his knee. The mother ran after the child who fell and took him in her arms. The child stopped crying. The man stopped yelling and held the mother who was holding the child. The other child came over and embraced the mother. They made a nice pose in full flesh and blood. The mother was wearing pink pointy shoes and the man wore boots. There you have it.

They danced in the moonlight.

They listened to French music on summer nights and had picnics at the light of the fireflies. They would go: "oh wow, look at the beautiful fireflies, it's like the stars fell in the grass." Poetic things like that.

One summer night the woman made love with a man who visited her, under the big tree in the backyard.

Was it the same man?

It doesn't matter, I told you, the men came and left, the woman stayed. The men were always different, the woman was the same woman.

She wore pink dresses on spring mornings.

She wore white dresses on summer afternoons.

She wore all the colors.

The children grew up and left. The woman cried a lot with the departure of each child.

They returned on holidays. They had holiday dinners and even made fires and sat by the fires telling stories.

The woman liked the snow, she came out on snowy nights and stared at the snowflakes. She whispered to them in different languages. She said the name of snow in all the languages she knew. She sniffled the air like a hungry she-wolf. She lay down on the snow and looked at the sky for a long time.

The children came out and called her. She said, *come out here and lay in the snow next to me. It's so beautiful. We might not have snow for a long time on earth, enjoy it while you can.*

The children listened to her and stretched out on the snow next to her and they lay like that for a long time.

Humans! They can be so wasteful of time.

Don't be judgmental. She loved us and cared for us.

What happened in the end?

The men left.

The children left.

She got old.

She ate very little, like a bird.

Yes, she was a bit of a bird. She was light.

What happened?

The big storms came and beat the house this way and that way. But the house still stood.

Then came a big flood, the waters climbed to the first floor, but she was on the second floor and lived. She wrote her stories in her bedroom and the house still stood.

Then came all the other plagues and everybody disappeared or died. She disappeared while writing a story. She entered inside her own story and was gone forever. Like dying in your sleep.

She was lucky.

She made her luck.

How long has it been?

Time is not important. It could be yesterday; it could be 500 years ago.

We came up with enough memories to bring them to life. Now it's up to them to want to come back to life.

Hmm, I'm tired, I've had a hard time today bringing back the family in the white house.

I'm tired too, so I'll sleep well tonight.

And while we sleep and dream, our memories will grow and bloom and in the morning they might all be here when we wake up.

Well said, we'll dream them into being and when we wake up, we'll see our dreams come true.

Dream hard, good night.

We all came back to life in watery forms with feathers and bird voices and restarted inhabiting the house for a new future. It all happened in the tense of the future in the past. It's a compound tense in all the languages I know.

House Number Two

My house number two is in the first country, the one I was born and grew up in. I've never owned it or rented it or built it, but it seems just as real. It's a house of *DOR*, the one I crave for in my sleep, the one I wished I had saved money for and bought on a whim, on a quick visit, a house to come back to and cuddle up with myself in fetal position to listen to the local birds and the vowels in my first language and eat the pastries in. It's the house I should have gotten hundreds of times on my travels back to this native country with Carpathians and Black Sea, and funny jokes and blood relatives some still living, and others buried in the cemetery on a grassy field with a view of my favorite mountain peak. It's a house of white stone and dark wood, so close to the mountain peak that you think the mountain might fall on it any minute or you might think it was built right into the mountain side. It doesn't have wide windows like the house number one but tiny windows to keep it cool in the summer and warm in the winter, framed by sills made of pine wood, like the floors in my house number one. Only this pine still smells like the pines on the mountain peaks, pines so tall that your eyes squint when you look at their tops and are all symmetrically lined up against the sky, a straight line of pine trees with perfectly lined up tops, and some of them ended up in the windowsills of my house number two.

When I visited this country during the apocalypse people warned me to hurry before it's too late, they said, they said: *better buy your house before it's too late, our country is bought by another, bigger country, we are poor and they are rich, our leaders corrupt and our agriculture to the ground, the tomatoes are injected with hormones and the humans with a vaccine that contains a microchip so the government knows your every move, no way in hell am I getting this vaccine, better die of the apocalypse, it's all going to hell, but the houses are cheap. Better buy one before they hike up the prices. They want to get rid of all the old people, that's why they started the apocalypse, nobody wants us, we are old and produce nothing and keep getting our lousy pensions, it's why they started the apocalypse, and the canicular temperatures, to kill all the old people, better buy your house now.*

They are funny people who speak my native language, with twisted imaginations and dark thoughts about anything from the fate of local tomatoes to the fires in the Amazon but I can't help loving them and wanting to go back. The house of *DOR* is empty and waiting for me to buy it and furnish it with period pieces, adorn it with gauzy curtains and tapestries embroidered on the loom by old women in the nearby mountain villages. The *DOR* howls through it like a mad wind stirring up the pine smells of the pine tree wood in the windowsills.

This house too is populated with characters that speak to each other in theatrical forms like in the house number one, only these characters are born of the souls of my ancestors who watched me grow up and climb the local trees and eat green plumps and ripe cherries from the neighbors' trees and fall in love on a mountain top in a torrential rain with a rainbow after it, on an afternoon like no other in the history of rainy afternoons with a rainbow after it on a mountain top and a kiss like no other in the middle of it all. These characters talk in some archaic form of my native language that I only skim the meaning off the top of the words hanging with heavy triphthongs. Because they were already dead when I ran these streets around the house and climbed the neighbors' trees and ate their green or ripe fruit, they still speak of me in the future, trying to protect me from falling off a tree, falling in love with the wrong person or flying away to another country, like the colossal one with my house number one in it. They are trying to make me replay my own past and naively think I can make changes to it like you make corrections with the red pencil on an essay I wrote. They say things like:

Woe is her rushing down that valley in the torrential rain, little girl, little girl,

you'll catch your death, o sa racesti si te imbolnavesti de moarte si de dor

du-te'napoi cat mai ai timp

you'll catch a cold and catch your death and catch the deadly DOR

Go back while you still can

N-asculta, e capoasa rau, face ce vrea,

She won't listen, she does what she wants, she does what she wants, obdurate girl that she is

She is like Paraschiva and like Vera, and like Nadia strong headed, obdurate woman, only doing what she wants and throwing herself into heartbreak and DOR and lifelong yearning

Good for her, good for her, she'll make her fortune, let her go …

She'll fall in love right after the rain

She'll break her heart like you break a dry twig, crack

She'll bite right into the rainbow and kiss the boy

Then she'll shame us all with her shameless love

She'll carry it to its death; she'll step on it and leave it all in rags

Good for her, good for her, she is the courageous one in the family

Others were courageous too, but not like her

Look at her run around with the boy in the rain and the rainbow and the snow

Lie with him anywhere she pleases with no shame

You would too if you were young and fierce like her

Maybe I would, I don't know

She is not like us, she is an odd one, like an odd bird

She dreams of faraway countries, she wants it all,

We only wanted a tiny bit of land with food on it,

She wants the world, and the world will crush her

Lasa fata sa-si faca soarta ei, ajunge departe

Leave the girl alone to live her fate, she'll get far

What did I tell you? She's done with us, she's gone

O sa vina-n vacanta

She'll come back on vacation

But only after a long, long time when her heart will bleed for this here piece of earth and the rainbow after the rain with the kiss in it

And then she'll write a book, I hear that's what she does out there, writes books

I hear nobody reads the books anymore, they are all in a box with a screen and you don't turn the pages

There are books, just in different form, maybe she'll remember us in one of her books

She will, she will, she was wild but always kept her word

And now she wants the little house to write her books in it to put it in the box with the screen

I told you she's a greedy one

She wants everything, and nothing is ever enough.

Let her have it, she earned it, she yearned enough for this here patch of grass,

she worked hard out there among strangers and the DOR caught up with her

The world is burning fast, I hear it's a new apocalypse out there

Ce-a fost a fost, acuma-i sfarsitul lumii

What's done is done, now is the end of the world

Incepe alta noua

A new one is starting, worlds end and start again, didn't you know that much after all you saw in one war and then peace, and then another war and then another peace, on and on, good thing we are dead and gone and buried in the cemetery on the hill

we were the last ones to get these locuri de veci, these burial places, spots, the last ones, too many living on the earth, too many dead under the earth

Lots died this year in the new apocalypse, and all she cares about is her pretty dresses si casa de sub munte, and the house under the mountain

Let her have it, let her have the house.

House Number Three

While my house number one is in country number two, and my house number two is in country number one, to make things upside down and inside out my house number three is in country number three as well, so there is no upside down there, a perfectly symmetrical match just to prove it that it is my ideal country where I should have been born in or run away to.

This house has a window to the Mediterranean where I swam deliriously drunk on its fierce blues when I was seventeen and in love with a Romanian boy whom I had left but who thought he had left me and it's just as well because he ended up as the male protagonist in my first novel. The Mediterranean where I swam with other loves and with my children on our vacations abroad from colossal country number two, and where I swam by myself for endless hours wanting to drink it and drown in it altogether, to become part of that dizzying liquid blue forever in a perpetual cosmic copulation. Through that window I see all my swims, from seventeen to fifty-seven, it's the window of swims in the Mediterranean. It's a house of white stone and red tiles roof, resembling the house in country number one, only made of better materials with more professional labor because this country number three was not pillaged by Communist and Fascist dictators and then sucked dry by foreign investors from Western countries such as this very country of my dreams with the windows looking out at the Mediterranean Sea.

This house keeps crumbling as it is being built, like the monastery from the ballad of the master builder whose monastery walls kept crumbling at night after he had built them during the day. Until one day when some angel spoke to him in a dream, and told him he had to build his own wife inside the walls of this special monastery ordered to him by the king of the country, of my country number one, where I was born and grew up and left one day without a goodbye on my big adventure to colossal country number two all while pining for magical country number three, of the upside down triangle tower.

Maybe in order to make this house looking out at the Mediterranean stand on its own and no longer collapse, I have to bury my own self inside it, and sit there quietly while the good laborers of this Western country, possibly all come from other countries in the East and all over the colonized globe, are laying brick on special brick leaving just enough openings for my special windows out to the blue, blue, demented turquoise sea. This special country of my dreams is asking for everything, for your every drop of blood and breath to give you a crumb of its land and air, it's the price you must pay for not having been born in it, for not having been part of its colonizers. Shame on you for being born on the wrong side of the world, of the colonizing lines!

When I visit this country of my dreams during this new apocalypse and ride this way and that way on its large boulevards with the view of the upside down triangle tower in the distance and people kissing each other with the autochthonous special kiss on every street, the drivers all come from far away, they are foreigners like me and they say things like "I don't feel like I belong here," "I don't feel like I am home here, but it's better than in my country which is corrupt and always at war." Another says "I want to go to your country, everything is big there, lots of room in the streets for the cars, not small and narrow like here." I say: "I wish

I stayed here in this country; I wish I was born here, this is my dream country." And they say "no, where you are is *my* dream country," they mean the colossal country where I have my wood-framed house with the piece of land and big tree in the back yard and all. The drivers and I commiserate over the state of the world, the apocalypse that is hovering everywhere, here they say the serum against the apocalypse will make you sterile, "you don't know what they put in it," "it's true, you don't but what are you going to do, you can't travel otherwise, you've got to take that damn serum if you want to do anything," I say, and I think *the world is overpopulated anyways, you don't need to make more children mister foreign driver living in my dream country.* I mentally slap myself for the bad thoughts towards this kind Uber driver, gloating at the possibility of his vaccine-induced sterility. I start talking to street vendors from Africa who sell key chains and refrigerator magnets with tiny Eiffel Tower amulets right next to the actual Eiffel Tower, and ask them how life has been for them lately, in this new apocalypse. I buy a handful of key chains and magnets as gifts for people back home, in my *de facto* home, my only real home, where my children grew up and where I write my books. They have nothing good to say, *"c'est dur, même plus dur maintenant,"* it's even harder now, the wait for immigration procedures and documents is endless, no hope, no light in sight, little or no access to health care, *more of us die of the disease than the white French, more of us get sick than the white French people.* I don't know what to say, I buy more Eiffel Tower key chains, I ask him if I can take a picture of him, of the group of them selling the ultimate, iconic image of Frenchness to Western tourists while their access to that coveted Frenchness is continuously denied. Not even before disease and death are African immigrants equal to the white locals.

When I say goodbye to this dream country after my travels during the apocalypse and I return to my second country with house number one in it, I know there is no way I am going to build myself inside the dream house with windows looking out at the Mediterranean, where African immigrants are just as unjustly treated as those in my country number two with house number one in it. Let it crumble. It will have to keep floating there like a perpetual hologram between the tower and the kiss. I am not giving it my blood and my body to be built inside it with all my veins and memory of magic swims and cumulated mortgages, and the scent of the Carpathians and memory of first love started on the slopes of those same fragrant Carpathians, no matter how much I dreamed of it when I was seventeen and thirty-seven and fifty-seven. And as I make this momentous decision about my house number three to never bring it into being except for in a holographic kind of way, I hear the voices of the ethereal characters in the backyard of my house number one in country number two, talking to each other in the tense of the future in the past and saying things like this:

She always came back here after each of her journeys, even after the journey during the apocalypse number three

She returned with new dresses and a brilliant manicure

She never bought the house in the foreign country by the Mediterranean

No, she didn't, she preferred this one

Who needs two or three houses anyways?

One house is enough, more than some other people who have none

She came out in the backyard wrapped in blue silks that shone like the sea

She danced in her blue silks like she swam in the sea

She went back in the white house and cried for a while

Then she stopped crying and called it the house of *DOR*.

Then she melted in her own story, but the silks remain to this day.

Rajiv Mohabir

An Antiman's Survival Despite[1]

I find myself puzzling over questions as we begin to wake from the haze of languishing in lockdowns, as the vaccination rollout is now making it possible for us to slowly come together again and share physical and psychic space once more. I don't have any answers to what it all means, and my realizations that I've learned to feel through my own body are made up of ancestral memory and muscle memory of times I've had my dignity challenged in the past, and what I've done to emerge from disaster with my eyes turned towards joy.

As I think about survival in this time of worldwide tragedy and death, it is not lost on me how it was Black, Indigenous, and People of Color (BIPOC) communities that faced a higher state of suffering and loss due to governments again failing us. What strength I draw from my situation where my entire world shifted into a state of alienated remoteness was what I could imagine through writing and reading; reflection and remembering the connections between all things—the connections between the forced migration of people, encounters with the Other, the disruption of colonization, and our current state of living in post-colonial fallout. Are these things connected? Every slightest bit of my affective reservoir: all of the pinprick hauntings of events, of every time the word *antiman* or *coolie* have been hurled at me or my family, those hauntings of fierce bigotry that cause my hair to stand on end say "yes."

I am currently living outside of Boston in Massachusetts in a town called Malden. What I have been writing about has been through fevered journals: the ways in which the United States perpetrates settler violence, how Massachusetts and the Caribbean have been in conversation of the forced migrations of African-descended people to Barbados and the imprisonment of the Wabenaki and Pawtucket people of Massachusetts and their involuntary relocation to the Caribbean. I am trying to name the strands of historical and personal hauntings that

---

1   Originally written as a keynote address delivered at "Live Pridefully: Love and Resilience Within Pandemics," Caribbean Equality Project (CEP), June 24, 2021. This essay was first published in *Stabroek News*.

informed my anxieties from March 2020—a March that feels like years ago. The Department of the Interior attempted to disband the Mashpee Reservation lands while neglecting the BIPOC communities hardest hit by Covid-19. What about queer organizing and community work? I have no answers, only questions that I present to you to illustrate how these traumas side by side have been profoundly disorganizing for me.

From wondering about the linkages between this pandemic, the roots of our inheritances, to the very damning of a people robbed of human dignities, I have returned to the idea that survival is who we Caribbean queers are. We suffered under legislation that has made our bodies, our desires, our unique ways of loving, criminal. We come from a long line of people who endured as seeds carried from foreign shores to where we are today. My own Guyanese family has four continents in our history: Asia, South America, Europe, and North America. Yet these lessons cause me to wonder about the homophobic hauntings that have taken root in my family causing pain and rupture. Being a queer in my family has not been an easy thing. Being told that I am an abomination and deserve to be shunned has deeply affected me. The time I was attacked in Union Square also haunts me. This pain is evident in the homophobia of our community as well. From Guyana's Criminal Law (Offences) Act and the maintenance of the colonial laws to our carrying these hatreds in our suitcases like *achar* into the United States, this poison seeps into our homes. This bigotry once hurt a friend dear to me: Zaman Amin who was brutally attacked outside of a club on Liberty Avenue. The irony is in the name, Liberty Avenue, where our rights to live are called into question.

And Zaman's spark was not tamped down but raged on through the fierce spirit of activism. When I left NYC to pursue my PhD in Honolulu the last thing that I did in the city was to attend a rally to bring attention and to seek justice for this attack in Richmond Hill. What moved me was to see the endurance of Zaman through their persona Sundari, the Indian goddess, who performed with a vigor that bore testament to radical, queer, paradigm-shattering joy. I was stirred by all of the people who came out to show support for our sibling. She has been a source of inspiration for me as she dances in public with a ferocity that won't be quelled, with a face that won't be ignored. In fact, for me, Sundari represents the opposite of the silencing hand of the cisgender heteropatriarchy, and I think of how much I admire her for her strength and how her truth serves as a torch to light small fires for us along the dark road of ignorance and deadly violence we encounter.

But this was not always the case, and the idea of resilience can be damaging to many. We are not supposed to endure. Shouldn't our elders and community lift us up as we all attempt to survive in this new country? Its costs drain us emotionally and psychically and scar us in ways that we will have to process for our lifetimes if we are privileged enough to find moments of respite and community. As a queer, I have lived through being cast out by my family—a loss of kin that I suffered greatly from. It felt as though I lost my kinfolk, my clan … it felt like I lost the only way I knew how to be in the world. I felt alone and fractured and did not in fact feel resilient. I write about this more fully in my memoir, *Antiman: A Hybrid Memoir* (Restless Books, 2021), and about how I survived the trauma of being cast out for being what my family called an antiman. I say this word, and I know its violence. I hear its shriek. It makes my stomach turn.

I hear it also as a question, a word that I can fully embrace to show a queerness that comes from Guyana, that has traveled across into Britishness, that has lived in the United States and in fact, points to a queerness that allows for the complexities: the concavities and convexities of our migration stories and ethnic heritages. Can I reclaim this word and marvel at the fact that it means that I am categorically against man or men? Can I be so brazen as to say that this word predicted that I would turn against the cisgender heteropatriarchy by being *ANTI* man? As I think through the devastation of this word, I love all of its avatars: ante-man, aunty-man, anti-man, and of course ant-y-man (a man with the power of an ant, which is quite strong for the ant's proportions).

I remember that telling my *aji* about the deepest part of myself, my love of another man, felt so outside of the realm of possibility—that I would rather die than admit to her that there was a cock in the fowl house. I imagined a world where I would be safe from the truth: that I could have a split life where there was an outside Rajiv and an inside Rajiv—as though I could only ever be only half a person at any one time—the other half of me hiding in shadow. In editing and rewriting this memoir in the time of the pandemic, I was able to see my story in a different perspective—from a glance where I already knew the outcome: that my *aji* would have a reaction completely different from what I imagined. Her grace and acceptance were unparalleled in my family.

And now, as the world opens its arms once more, as NYC through vaccination opens itself, I find myself back to the city where I learned to be whole, the very place I relearned how to be West Indian but this time without my Guyanese family that lived in Queens. I want to celebrate the broken sidewalks of Richmond Hill and Ozone Park where I saw metaphors for my own survival: bora growing wildly in gardens, backyard parties where queers danced with queers to chutney soca. To Sundari. To all the antiman kind. To kissing a boyfriend to Babla and Kanchan at a Chutney Pride event. I want to praise the poetry of our elders with gold teeth. I want to praise the "J" and "E" trains to Jamaica. I want to do this because every celebration is a celebration of now. I don't want to put off my life any longer but wish to live wholly. If this whole pandemic has taught me anything, it was that life is for now. That the time to sway with joy is this very instant.

So, I say to you all, celebrate the very magic that cast us into bodies: to that very music that beats within us. We don't have to wait for a time when we will all be "equal" in the eyes of the law. That day is not here now. We are here now with our queernesses, our kinks, our desires, and our Sundaris. Look around you for the things that will help you to keep going, to keep crossing despite the government's need to destitute us in America, despite being unwanted in our own Caribbean countries. We are forging a new bravery, built through our disjoints and fissures, that is infinitely fertile.

The things that I have learned about my own resilience during the pandemic was that I am stronger when I have others around me, we are stronger together—even through video conferencing. We find new ways to meaningfully connect to one another. In some ways this was the least alone I've ever felt. In some ways … I realized that I need people. That I need to celebrate joy more deliberately. That being Caribbean means that we are a people forged through destitution and colonization and that we are galvanized twice over—made stronger by all of the constituent elements that bring us our beauty and sturdiness. I have learned that yes, I am queer, an antiman, and this is my strength. This is our brown and black power, a force that when untied can never be brought down no matter how many bottles they smash on our heads. That we will be there to hold one another. Remember, we are the children of adventurers and survivors. We have reclaimed our humanity when it was stripped away. We are adaptable and we are goddam beautiful magic.

Visual Expressions

Octavio Quintanilla

Los días oscuros 91

The poem in Spanish can be translated as: When I open my eyes / I see myself with those of a fish / I want to swim in a desert / swim in a tree's crown / to sleep upside down / I close my eyes again / chew my face off.

Los días oscuros 113

The poem in Spanish can be translated as: Close your mouth. / The world rests in your eyes. / Don't say anything. / The grasshopper that sings to me in winter / is here.

Los días oscuros 293

The poem in Spanish can be translated as: Your gaze is a wire / necklace that chokes / I want to see / with the colors / you scream out.

Najmeh Hoseini

Yara

Oil color, 11 inches × 14 inches / 280 mm × 355 mm. Hoseini writes: "This piece was made in the summer of 2020 when the world shut down. The creative spirit woke me up at 5a.m. to create it. It happened so quickly and effortlessly, I was in awe." This is a depiction of Yara Sayeh Shahidi as a child. Shahidi is an Iranian African American actress, model, and activist.

Parallel Space

Oil color, 11 inches × 16 inches / 280 mm × 405 mm. This painting is inspired by the heartbreaking loss of lives to systemic racism and police brutality in the US. The artist states: "Before creating this piece, I drew parallel lines to give myself guidance for the figure's angles and the content of the spainting. By the end, I left the lines in to add depth to the painting."

ᐃURᐃ etc

que sera sera

Mixed media: marker drawing and acrylic painting. The painting depicts different scenes from individual existence, challenged by contradictions and split instances that paradoxically come together in a fair harmonious shape like a cave painting.

who & who

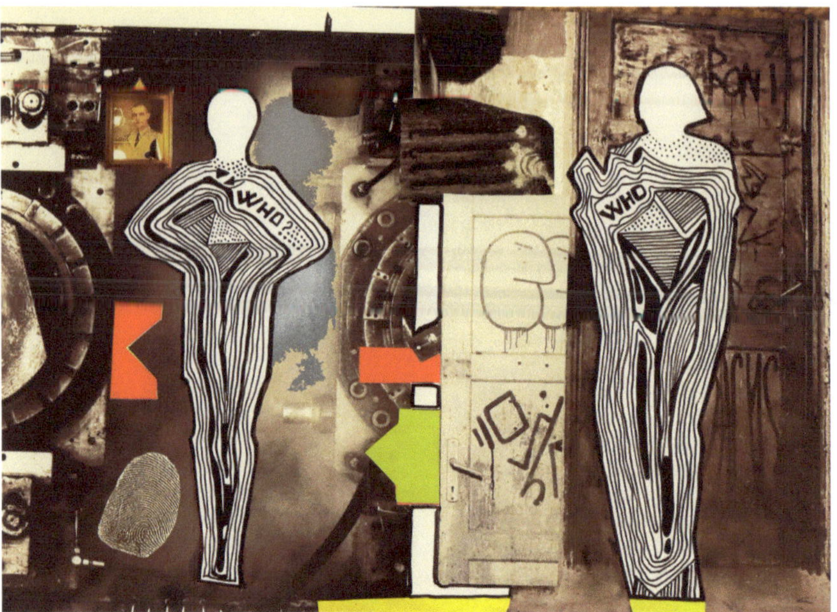

Mixed media: analogue collage and marker drawing. This collage depicts the anonymous precious existence in its urban and modest daily habitat.

historically sync.

Mixed media: analogue collage. This collage brings together different scenes of human history to redeem the potential of the individual mind to acknowledge so much in a short dream-like gesture. The result? Empathy and the transformative power of the conscious and subconscious at work.

Biographies

N.S. Bala is a writer based out of Reno, Nevada. An immigrant, whose life and family spans across the globe, she writes primarily about the South Asian transnational experience. She also likes to experiment with comedy and is currently working on a comedic screenplay.

Before teaching at the University of Oklahoma, **Roxana L. Cazan** taught literature, creative writing, and women's studies courses at Saint Francis University in Pennsylvania. She is an interpreter and translator of Romanian, and a poet. Her poems have been featured in *Poets Reading the News*, *The Windsor Review*, *Cold Creek Review*, *Construction Literary Magazine*, *Glass Lyre Press*, *Adanna Literary Journal*, *Watershed Review*, *The Portland Review*, *Harpur Palate*, and others. Her full-length poetry books are *The Accident of Birth* (Main Street Rag, 2017) and *Tethered to the Unexpected* (Alien Buddha Press, 2022). Roxana's scholarly work focuses on ethnic and post-colonial literature and women's studies and has appeared in *Neophilologus*, *Women's Studies Quarterly*, *Comparative Literature Studies*, *Studies in American Jewish Literature*, *American Journal of Undergraduate Research*, and others. She is the author of a chapter included in *Remembering Kahina: Women, Representation and Resistance in Post-Independence North Africa* (Routledge, 2022), a chapter included in the anthology *Mothers, Mothering, and Globalization* (Demeter Press, 2017), and the co-editor of the anthology, *Voices on the Move: An Anthology by and about Refugees* (Solis Press, 2020). She currently serves as Diversity, Equity, and Inclusion Specialist at a *Fortune* 500 company.

Lucia Cherciu is the author of five books of poetry, including *Train Ride to Bucharest* (Sheep Meadow Press, 2017), a winner of the Eugene Paul Nassar Poetry Prize. She is the 2021 Dutchess County Poet Laureate, and her work was nominated three times for a Pushcart Prize and twice for Best of the Net. She teaches English at SUNY/Dutchess in Poughkeepsie, NY. Currently, she is working on revising her novel. Her web page is at http://luciacherciu.webs.com. You can also find her on Twitter: @CherciuLucia.

Julia Kolchinksy Dasbach emigrated from Ukraine as a Jewish refugee when she was six years old. She is the author of three poetry collections: *The Many Names for Mother*, winner of the Wick Poetry Prize (Kent State University Press, 2019), finalist for the Jewish Book Award; *Don't Touch the Bones* (Lost Horse Press, 2020), winner of the 2019 Idaho Poetry Prize; and *40 WEEKS* (forthcoming from YesYes Books, 2023). Her recent poems appear in *Blackbird*, *American Poetry Review*, and *The Nation*, among others. Julia is the editor of *Construction Magazine*. She holds an MFA from the University of Oregon and a PhD in Comparative Literature from the University of Pennsylvania. She is the new Murphy Fellow in Poetry at Hendrix College and recently relocated to Little Rock, Arkansas with her two kids, a cat, a dog, and a husband. You can find her on Twitter: @JKDPoetry.

Cătălina Florina Florescu is a Romanian-born American interdisciplinary scholar and writer. At Pace University in New York City, she teaches learning community, honors courses in literature, cultural studies, cinema, and writing. She developed three new courses, all focusing on theater: twenty-first century dramatic texts as intercultural dialogue; worlds in literature: immigration and Englishes; and women in literature: theater of resistance. She is an author whose books are in permanent libraries worldwide as well as at the Library of Congress in Washington, DC.: *Transacting Sites of the Liminal Bodily Spaces* (literary criticism; medical humanities); *Disjointed Perspectives on Motherhood* (mothers in literature and motion picture; feminist criticism); *Inventing Me/Exerciţii de retrăit* (memoir); *Transnational Narratives in Englishes of Exile* (cultural and literary criticism; immigration; Englishes and plurality; diversity and diaspora studies). The year 2017 also marked her debut in poetry with a volume titled, *The Night I Burned My Origami Skin*. Her plays have been performed and published internationally.

Najmeh (Naj) Hoseini was born and raised in Iran and worked as a physical therapist there before moving to the US in pursuit of a PhD in Indiana University in 2009. She completed her PhD studies with a focus on neuroplasticity with a major in kinesiology and a minor in neuroscience. She is currently a faculty at West Coast University in Los Angeles. Naj started painting in 2015 when she was a full-time faculty member at Midwestern University in Arizona. Naj has always been passionate about art and especially painting since childhood and the pandemic provided her with more spare time to focus on working on her craft as an artist. She held an art-show/fundraising for Phoenix Dream Center in August 2021 in collaboration with a physical therapy clinic in Arizona. Since then, she has built up her website and social media presence and has sold many pieces inside and outside of the US. She is very passionate about the well-being and freedom of women and respect for wildlife.

Amy M. Le was born in Vietnam nine months before the fall of Saigon and immigrated to the US at the age of five with her mother and cousin. Like hundreds of thousands of boat people, her family fled Vietnam as refugees of the war to escape persecution. Because Amy was also born with a congenital heart defect (CHD), the escape was extremely perilous and complicated due to her condition. In 1980, her family was sponsored to live in America. After graduating from Western Washington University with a BA in Sociology, Amy served for twenty years in the tech industry before taking the plunge to become a full-time writer. She is the author of the Snow trilogy: *Snow in Vietnam*, *Snow in Seattle*, and *Snow's Kitchen*. Amy is also the founder of Quill Hawk Publishing and helps authors to indie publish their work. To continue her passion for community service, Amy co-founded The Heart Community Collection, an online cooperative bookstore for the CHD community. She also partners with Together For Good Refugee Film School, Healing Hearts Vietnam, the Vietnamese Heritage Museum, the Spero Project, and the Seahawks Booster Clubs. Amy is a member of several organizations including the Asian Author Alliance, the Pacific Northwest Writers Association, Oklahoma City Writers, Inc., Oklahoma Writers Federation, Inc., Telltale Authors, the Yukon Writers' Society, and the Alliance of Independent Authors (ALLi). For fun, Amy loves to cook, watch NFL, UFC, and F-1 events.

Joan Lipkin is an internationally recognized writer, director, educator, and social activist currently based in St. Louis, as the producing artistic director of That Uppity Theatre Company, Dance the Vote, and Playback Now! St. Louis. Joan specializes in creating original devised works promoting dialogue and civic engagement. She has worked extensively with diverse populations including the LGBTQIA+ community, people with Alzheimer's and early-onset dementia, people with disabilities, women who have been sexually trafficked, people in recovery, college students, cancer patients, immigrants, inner-city youth, and communities of faith. Her work has been widely anthologized and produced. Other recent publications include blogs for HowlRound, the H.E.A.T. Collective and Stages of Resistance. Recent and current projects include creating work around the pandemic, producing plays as part of the international Climate Change Theatre Action, co-producing "Every 28 Hours" and "After Orlando", co-producing the Midwest premiere of "26 Pebbles" about the Sandy Hook massacre, creating the Queer Cafe for intentional conversation in Belgrade, Serbia. Awards include a Visionary, Ethical Humanist of the Year, Leadership for Community-based Theatre and Civic Engagement, a Woman of Achievement, What's Right with the Region, and IDEA, among many others.

Annie Lulu was born in Iasi, Romania to a Congolese father and a Romanian mother. Arriving in France at a very young age, she studied philosophy, then devoted herself entirely to writing. She is the author of two novels: *La Mer Noire dans les Grands Lacs* (Éditions Julliard, 2021) and *Peine des Faunes* (Éditions Julliard, 2022). *La Mer Noire dans les Grands Lacs* received the Prix Senghor, the Jean Cocteau prize, the Alain Fournier prize and the Prix de la Littérature de l'exil. *Peine des Faunes* received the Prix du Roman écologique. She is a PhD candidate in francophone studies at Johns Hopkins University.

Monica Manolachi is a lecturer of English and Spanish at the University of Bucharest, Romania. *Performative Identities in Contemporary Caribbean British Poetry* (Ars Docendi, 2017) is part of her work as a researcher and literary critic. She has published numerous academic articles on contemporary poetry and prose, including "Multiethnic resonances in Derek Walcott's poetry", in *Ethnic Resonances in Performance, Literature, and Identity* (Routledge, 2019). Her poems have appeared in *The Blue Nib* (USA), *WordCityLit* (Canada), *Artemis Poetry* (UK), *Culture Cult* (India), *DLITE, Crevice, Poetry Stand, Contemporary Literary Horizon* (Romania), and others. In 2018, she co-authored the bilingual poetry collection *Brasília* (PIM, 2018) with Scottish poet Neil Leadbeater. She also published the bilingual anthology *Joining the Dots* (PIM, 2016) and, in Romanian, *Poveștile Fragariei către Magul Viridis* (Brumar, 2012) and *Trandafiri* (Lumen, 2007). She is a member of ARTLIT, the Romanian Association of Literary Translators.

Rajiv Mohabir is the author of *Cutlish* (Four Way Books, 2021, finalist for the 2022 National Book Critics Circle Award, longlisted for the 2022 PEN/Voelcker Award for Poetry), *The Cowherd's Son* (Tupelo Press, 2017, winner of the 2015 Kundiman Prize; Eric Hoffer Honorable Mention 2018) and *The Taxidermist's Cut* (Four Way Books, 2016, winner of the Four Way Books Intro to Poetry Prize, Finalist for the Lambda Literary Award for Gay Poetry in 2017), and translator of *I Even Regret Night: Holi Songs of Demerara (1916)* (Kaya Press, 2019, which received a PEN/Heim Translation Fund Grant Award and the 2020 Harold Morton Landon Translation Award from the Academy of American Poets). His memoir *Antiman* (Restless Books, 2021, finalist for the PEN Open Book Award, and the 2022 Publishing Triangle Randy Shilts Award and the Lambda Literary Award for Gay Memoir), received the 2019 Restless Books Prize for New Immigrant Writing. Currently he is an assistant professor of Poetry in the MFA program at Emerson College and the translations editor at *Waxwing Journal.*

Luisa Muradyan is originally from Ukraine and holds a PhD in Poetry from the University of Houston where she was the recipient of an Inprint Jesse H. and Mary Gibbs Jones Fellowship and a College of Liberal Arts and Sciences Dissertation Fellowship. She is the author of *American Radiance* (University of Nebraska Press) and was the editor-in-chief of *Gulf Coast: A Journal of Literature and Fine Arts* from 2016 to 2018. She was also the recipient of the 2017 Prairie Schooner Book Prize and the 2016 Donald Barthelme Prize in Poetry. Forthcoming poems can be found at the *Threepenny Review*, *Poetry London*, *The Iowa Review*, and *PANK* among others.

Octavio Quintanilla is the author of the poetry collection, *If I Go Missing* (Slough Press, 2014) and served as the 2018–2020 poet laureate of San Antonio, Texas. His poetry, fiction, translations, photography, and Frontextos (visual poems) have appeared, or are forthcoming, in many journals. Octavio's visual work has been exhibited in several galleries throughout the United States. He holds a PhD from the University of North Texas and is the regional editor for *Texas Books in Review* and poetry editor for *The Journal of Latina Critical Feminism* and for *Voices de la Luna: A Quarterly Literature & Arts Magazine*. Octavio teaches Literature and Creative Writing in the MA/MFA program at Our Lady of the Lake University in San Antonio, Texas.

Domnica Radulescu is an American writer of Romanian origin, living in the United States where she arrived in 1983 as a political refugee, having escaped the communist dictatorship of her native Romania. She settled in Chicago where she obtained a master's degree in Comparative Literature and a PhD in Romance Languages from the University of Chicago. She is the Edwin A. Morris Professor of Comparative Literature at Washington & Lee University. Radulescu is the author of three critically acclaimed novels, *Train to Trieste* (Knopf, 2008 & 2009), *Black Sea Twilight* (Transworld, 2011 & 2012) and *Country of Red Azaleas* (Hachette, 2016) and of award-winning plays. *Train to Trieste* has been published in thirteen languages and is the winner of the 2009 Library of Virginia Fiction Award. Radulescu received the 2011 Outstanding Faculty Award from the State Council of Higher Education for Virginia and is twice a Fulbright scholar. Radulescu also published fourteen non-fiction books, edited and coedited collections on topics ranging from the tragic heroine in Western literature to feminist comedy, to studies of exile literature to theater of war and exile, refugee art, and two collections of original plays. Two of her plays, *Exile Is My Home* and *The Town with Very Nice People* were runners up for the Jane Chambers Playwriting award in 2012 and 2013. *Dream in a Suitcase: The Story of an Immigrant Life* is her first memoir (Austin Macauley, 2021).

Ellen Scherer is a writer, director, and cofounder of Green Buffalo Productions (GBP), based in Buffalo, New York. Recent publications include *I've Got Nothing* (Too Well Away), *A Year of Fruit* (Spirited Muse Press), *I'll Drink to That* (The Literatus), and *RCVI: Gun Violence* (Rosen Publishing). Other writing credits include *2020 Was My Year* (A Moment of Your Time), *When the Party's Over* (Cone Man Running), *I Was Here* (Equity Library Theatre, Open Space Arts, Inclusive Theatre of WNY), *I've Got Your Back* (GBP), *Scary Monsters* (GBP, Inclusive Theatre of WNY). Ellen has directed and produced several pieces for GBP over the past three years and has recently added to her bag of tricks as a film editor for the company's Spooky Film Festival. You can also find her on Instagram: @green_bflo.

Claudia Serea is a Romanian-born poet with poems and translations published in *Field, New Letters, Prairie Schooner, The Puritan, Oxford Poetry,* and elsewhere. She is the author of seven poetry collections, most recently *In Those Years, No One Slept* (Broadstone Books, 2023) and *Writing on the Walls at Night* (Unsolicited Press, 2022). Serea won the Joanne Scott Kennedy Memorial Prize from the Poetry Society of Virginia, the *New Letters* Readers Award, and the Franklin-Christoph Award. Her poems have been translated in French, Italian, Russian, Arabic, and Farsi, and featured on *The Writer's Almanac*. She is a founding editor of *National Translation Month*, serves on the board of the Red Wheelbarrow Poets, and co-hosts their monthly readings.

Born in Birmingham, England, **Sandra Soli** emigrated to Oklahoma after the second world war and became a naturalized American citizen while attending Oklahoma College for Women. After a lengthy career in broadcasting, she graduated *magna cum laude* in Communications, then completed an honors MA in English at the University of Central Oklahoma. Sandy has served as a visiting lecturer at regional universities and is a popular speaker at writing conferences. Her work has been featured on National Public Radio, nominated for the AWP Intro Award, and the prestigious Pushcart Prize. Her chapbook, *Silvering the Flute*, finalist for the Oklahoma Book Award, sold out of two printings. Her new chapbook, *What the Trees Know*, is the 2008 recipient of the Oklahoma Book Award.

Alina Stefanescu was born in Romania and lives in Birmingham, Alabama with her partner and several intense mammals. Recent books include a creative nonfiction chapbook, *Ribald* (Bull City Press Inch Series, 2020). Her poetry collection, *dor*, won the Wandering Aengus Press Prize in 2021. Alina's writing can be found (or is forthcoming) in diverse journals, including *Prairie Schooner, North American Review, World Literature Today, Pleiades, FLOCK, Southern Humanities Review, Crab Creek Review*, and others. She serves as poetry editor for *Pidgeonholes*, poetry editor for *Random Sample Review, Poetry Reviewer for Up the Staircase Quarterly*, and co-director of PEN America's Birmingham Chapter. More online at www.alinastefanescuwriter.com.

Anna Veprinska is the author of the full-length poetry collection *Sew with Butterflies* (Steel Bananas, 2014); the chapbooks *Stone Blossom* (Anstruther Press, 2022) and *Spirit-clenched* (Gap Riot Press, 2020); and the monograph *Empathy in Contemporary Poetry after Crisis* (Palgrave Macmillan, 2020), which received Honourable Mention in the Memory Studies Association First Book Award. Her poetry was shortlisted for the 2021 Austin Clarke Prize in Literary Excellence and was finalist for Best of the Net in 2022. Her poems have been published in *Not Very Quiet: The Anthology* (Recent Work Press, 2021), as well as the journals *Arc Poetry Magazine, Parentheses, Hamilton Arts & Letters, The /tɛmz/ Review, Not Very Quiet, 8 Poems,* and *Echolocation,* among others. She holds a SSHRC-funded PhD in English from York University, where she was awarded the dissertation prize, and a master's in English from the University of Oxford. She is an assistant professor of English at Cape Breton University and an immigrant-settler living in Sydney, Nova Scotia.

Alexander Weinstein is the author of the short story collections, *Universal Love* and *Children of the New World.* His fiction and interviews have appeared in *Rolling Stone, World Literature Today, Best American Science Fiction & Fantasy,* and *Best American Experimental Writing.* He is a recipient of a Sustainable Arts Foundation Award, and has been awarded the Lamar York, Gail Crump, Hamlin Garland, and New Millennium Prizes. He is the founder and director of The Martha's Vineyard Institute of Creative Writing and a professor of Creative Writing at Siena Heights University.